READY FOR ANYTHING

Four Touchstones for
Future-Focused
Learning

SUZETTE LOVELY

foreword by Sean Covey

Solution Tree | Press

a division of
Solution Tree

555 North Morton Street
Bloomington, IN 47404
800.733.6786 (toll free) / 812.336.7700
FAX: 812.336.7790

email: info@SolutionTree.com
SolutionTree.com
Visit **go.SolutionTree.com/21stcenturyskills** to download the free reproducibles in this book.

Printed in the United States of America

Library of Congress Cataloging-in-Publication Data

Names: Lovely, Suzette, 1958- author.
Title: Ready for anything : four touchstones for future-focused learning /
    Suzette Lovely.
Description: Bloomington, Indiana : Solution Tree Press, 2019. | Includes
    bibliographical references and index.
Identifiers: LCCN 2019005402 | ISBN 9781947604391
Subjects: LCSH: Education--Aims and objectives. | Effective teaching. |
    School-to-work transition. | Educational innovations. | Culturally
    relevant pedagogy. | Individualized instruction.
Classification: LCC LB1025.3 .L696 2019 | DDC 370--dc23 LC record available at https://
lccn.loc.gov/2019005402

Solution Tree
Jeffrey C. Jones, CEO
Edmund M. Ackerman, President

Solution Tree Press
President and Publisher: Douglas M. Rife
Associate Publisher: Sarah Payne-Mills
Art Director: Rian Anderson
Managing Production Editor: Kendra Slayton
Production Editor: Alissa Voss
Senior Editor: Amy Rubenstein
Copy Editor: Miranda Addonizio
Proofreader: Elisabeth Abrams
Text and Cover Designer: Laura Cox
Editorial Assistant: Sarah Ludwig

Acknowledgments

Solution Tree Press would like to thank the following reviewers:

Scott Carr
Principal
Heritage Middle School
Liberty, Missouri

Daniel Cohan
Community Superintendent
Jefferson County Public School District
Golden, Colorado

Christopher Eberlein
Principal
Speegleville Elementary School
Waco, Texas

Mike Hagadone
Deputy Superintendent
White River School District
Buckley, Washington

Mary Hendricks-Harris
Superintendent
Francis Howell School District
St. Charles, Missouri

Marsha Jones
Executive Director, Curriculum and
Instruction
Pasadena Independent School District
Pasadena, Texas

Amanda Ziaer
Principal
Hunt Middle School
Frisco, Texas

Visit **go.SolutionTree.com/21stcenturyskills** to download the free reproducibles in this book.

Table of Contents

About the Author vii

Foreword ix

Introduction 1
    The Four Touchstones 1
    In This Book 2

1   Rethinking Education **5**
    The Changing Paradigm of Schooling 6
    Vital Skills for a Changing Economy 8
    A Farewell to Average 9
    The Any-Collar Workforce 10
    Future-Ready Teaching and Learning 13
    Constructive Rebellion Against Conformity 15
    Conclusion: There Is No Limit for Better .16
    Touchstone Takeaways 17

2   Implementing Innovative Practices **21**
    Six Characteristics of Innovative Educators 23
    Eight Themes of Practical DREAMING 24
    Strategies to Increase Innovation in the Student Environment 26
    Conclusion: Take a Walk on the Dog Side of Life 35
    Touchstone Takeaways 35

3   **Building a Strengths-Based Culture**. **39**

Focusing on Strong Versus Wrong 41

Developing Leadership in Teachers and Students. 44

Encouraging the Zookeeper Effect. 48

Creating Defining Moments 50

Molding Mindsets—Theirs and Ours 55

Conclusion: Wise Up. 58

Touchstone Takeaways 59

4   **Designing Personalized Experiences** **63**

Seven Questions to Kickstart the Process 64

Core Components of Personalization. 66

Strategies for Designing Personalized Experiences 69

Conclusion: Settle or Soar 77

Touchstone Takeaways 79

5   **Collaborating With the Outside**. **83**

Education Philanthropy Through the Ages 84

The Collective Impact Movement 86

Collaborating With Millennial Parents 94

Conclusion: Lower the Drawbridge 99

Touchstone Takeaways 100

Epilogue. **105**

Assess Your Identity. 105

Turn Words Into a Movement 107

Conclusion: A New Hope 107

Appendix **109**

Carlsbad Unified School District Graduate Profile 110

Lakeside Union School District Graduate Profile 111

References and Resources **113**

Index **123**

About the Author

 **Suzette Lovely, EdD,** spent thirty-four years serving K–12 schools in every capacity—from instructional aide to teacher to principal to central office administrator to superintendent. During her role as superintendent in Carlsbad, California, she spearheaded several efforts to support future-ready learning, including the implementation of a career pathways grant involving eighteen school districts throughout San Diego County; coordination of workforce readiness meetings with community college presidents, elected officials, and business leaders; and participation in collective impact endeavors with nonprofits. Dr. Lovely was also one of a handful of superintendents invited to participate in a focus group with California's governor to discuss the state's new funding and accountability system.

Since retiring, Dr. Lovely has remained active in strategic planning work, superintendent searches, leadership coaching, university teaching, and facilitation of the Women in Education Leadership (WEL) Institute. Dr. Lovely has been recognized for her visionary leadership and educational contributions by California Senator Patricia Bates, the California PTA, Hi-Noon Rotary, the Carlsbad Chamber of Commerce, *The Master Teacher* publication, and the San Diego County Art Education Association.

Dr. Lovely is the author of three books: *Staffing the Principalship, Setting Leadership Priorities*, and *Generations at School*. She has also authored numerous journal articles on capacity building and leadership development. Dr. Lovely has been a featured speaker at several local, state, and national conferences.

Following her undergraduate work at the University of California, Irvine, Dr. Lovely earned a master's degree in educational administration from National University and a doctorate from California State University, Fullerton. Her doctoral research provides unique insights into the generational perspectives of Millennial teachers and their long-term commitment to the profession.

To learn more about Dr. Lovely's work, email dr.suzette.lovely@gmail.com, or follow @SuzetteLovely on Twitter. To book Suzette Lovely for professional development, contact pd@SolutionTree.com.

Foreword

by Sean Covey

It is both an honor and a pleasure to write the foreword for this tremendous book by Dr. Suzette Lovely. Although we don't know each other well, her reputation precedes her, and I have the greatest respect for the decades of her life she has devoted to education. Having worked in all educational roles and capacities during this time (from teacher's aide to educator, principal, and then California superintendent), Dr. Lovely truly walks her talk. What, then, has led her to connect with me?

I am also in the education business. And although I come from quite a different background (having never been an official teacher or received a PhD), I spend my life in a classroom of sorts. I study kids—their behavior, ideas, opinions, and more. And as president of the FranklinCovey Education division, mentoring future-ready learners is also my passion. Several years back, I published a book (following in my father's footsteps) called *The 7 Habits of Highly Effective Teens*. Following a decade of research, I concluded that our current education system is just not keeping up with the needs of today's students. This led my division at FranklinCovey to bring forth a character-based curriculum of its own, *The Leader in Me*. We saw the need and knew that something needed to be done.

Which brings me to Dr. Lovely. I am enormously gratified by her courageous leadership in identifying ways to bring our current school systems and educators into the new millennium. The time has come to shift away from the paradigms of the past and embrace the future. In *Ready for Anything: Four Touchstones for Future-Focused Learning*, Dr. Lovely introduces us to her education model, comprised of four touchstones or criteria which can help point educators toward meaningful adjustments that will help prepare our children for the future. These four touchstones are remarkable, proven principles that work wherever a student or teacher falls in their educational journey. Let me explain by giving a quick preview of these principles.

First, Dr. Lovely stresses the need for *implementing innovative practices*. Mahatma Gandhi said, "The future depends on what we do in the present." This touchstone encourages educators to challenge students to innovate and create through new ideas and practices. When they do this, they take a big step into the future.

The second touchstone describes how important it is to *build a strengths-based culture*. This is accomplished by talking to students about their interests and ideas and helping them utilize their innate talents. This, in turn, can lead to new discoveries and build confident learners of the future.

The third touchstone explains the importance of *designing personalized experiences* for each and every student. There is no one-size-fits-all approach to learning. Students must be individually considered and given what they personally need to progress in their own time and their own way.

Fourth, Dr. Lovely believes in the vital importance of *collaborating with the outside*. Communities, organizations, parents, and others help shape, mold, and connect students to their own unique environments. It truly takes a village.

Each of these touchstones frames a future-ready learning process that advances the cutting edge of education. As Abraham Lincoln once said, "The best way to predict the future is to create it." I believe Dr. Lovely is doing just that. By providing this forward-looking framework, she invites educators everywhere to utilize these tools in the way that works best for their situation. I believe it's time that we take a good look at what's happening around us in technology, with the internet, social media, and the economy. It is so important to recognize that today's students need to be prepared to face the reality of a changing world. We can no longer sit back wearing our old lenses and think all is well. A new prescription is needed. Students are ready and waiting for us to guide them into the future. I wholeheartedly support Dr. Lovely's efforts to aid in this process and highly endorse *Ready for Anything* as a crucial catalyst for implementing these changes.

Introduction

Renowned 20th century inventor and designer Buckminster Fuller said you can't change things by fighting the existing system. Rather, to change something, you need to build new models that make existing models obsolete (Buckminster Fuller Institute, n.d.). Fuller spent his life working across disciplines to make the world better for humankind. His broad perspective on global problems drew him to pioneer solutions that revolutionized how people thought, connected, and lived.

This book is designed to inspire educators to become the Buckminster Fullers of their craft—to be lifelong learners, to continuously refine their practice, and to give learners the space to explore and dream. To prepare future-ready learners, learning, not teaching, must serve as the focal point for action. Throughout the pages of the book, I offer readers a compelling picture of a future-ready learner. In each chapter, I present practical approaches to create enriching experiences that feed students' minds, curiosity, and aspirations. The impetus of the book is to encourage all educators to motivate and exhilarate learners from kindergarten year to senior year so that we prepare youngsters for life beyond high school. We know that we can't reserve the most joyful learning experiences for the elementary grades; middle and high school students crave these opportunities too. At the same time, discussions about what students want to be when they grow up can't wait until high school.

The Four Touchstones

This book introduces four touchstones to help readers reimagine their work (figure I.1, page 2). A *touchstone* is a standard or criterion by which something is judged, and it serves as a barometer for assessing the quality of the work educators do. Each touchstone provides a method and means to enable students to function well in school, the workplace, and life. The point is to initiate meaningful changes that lead to better opportunities for students. The touchstone model is a fitting construct for K–12 teachers, administrators, counselors, curriculum coaches, and professional development coordinators who are on a mission to prepare future-ready learners.

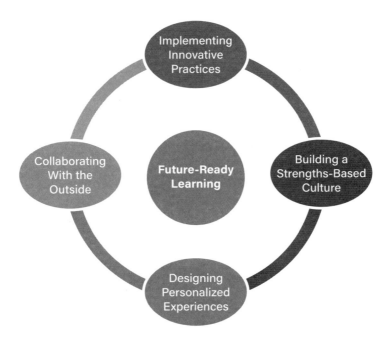

Figure I.1: The four touchstones of future-ready learning.

In This Book

Chapter 1 lays the foundation for the book by taking a deep look at a new paradigm of schooling. Included in this chapter are adjustments to teaching and learning that reflect what's happening technologically, socially, economically, and globally. As you'll discover in chapter 1, every institution in society is facing a reset. You'll be reminded of the economic realities students face when they leave high school and how these realities have shifted our responsibilities.

Chapter 2 examines the first touchstone: *implementing innovative practices.* Innovation occurs when we try something new (invention) or make an existing practice better (reinvention). Through fluid thinking, we can solve novel instructional challenges independent of any methods used in the past. While pockets of innovation have always existed in schools, this touchstone focuses on the disruptive practices that spawn new ideas and unforgettable experiences. This chapter introduces approaches from outside education to broaden readers' perspectives. The emphasis of this chapter is to help readers take students to levels of learning they never thought possible.

Chapter 3 delves into the elements of *building a strengths-based culture* and how a growth mindset feeds it. As educators foster students' strengths, interests, talents, and leadership potential, learners feel valued and successful. Within this touchstone are common language strategies and vignettes that propel teams toward a strengths-based environment. This chapter presents methods to fit various settings to allow readers to tap into what's already in place in their own building or district.

Chapter 4 investigates pathways to *designing personalized experiences*. Personalization refers to instruction that is paced to learner needs and preferences. This touchstone focuses on instruction becoming something we do *with* students, rather than *to* students. Crucial questions along with authentic examples offer readers insights and inspiration that ensure every learner can thrive.

Chapter 5 uncovers proven strategies to guide schools in successfully *collaborating with the outside*. Within this touchstone are structures and systems to enlist meaningful involvement from external and internal partners, including nonprofit agencies, philanthropic donors, the business community, and Millennial parents. Measures to connect students and teachers to local employers, industry experts, and outside professionals will create a lasting impact.

Rounding out each chapter are Touchstone Takeaways, which include Points to Ponder and Rapid-Fire Ideas to allow readers to gain immediate traction with the strategies they implement. Throughout the book, readers will discover stories and perspectives from the field so that site-level and district teams can walk the path to future-focused teaching and learning together.

It's important to note that this book is not intended to provide step-by-step instructions to get a school district from point A to point B. If you're expecting a prescriptive user's guide to innovation, strengths-based environments, personalization, or external collaboration, you may be disappointed. Every school and district will have a different starting and ending place based on student needs, work culture, organizational leadership, and current priorities. Rather, think of this book as a road map with a plethora of routes to reach your destination. Whether you take a direct path or follow a more meandering course, this book is meant to be a flexible planning tool to synchronize individual and team efforts.

Remarkable things are happening in classrooms, schools, and central offices across the globe. By sharing these remarkable things, it is my hope to tilt education practices away from adult interests and desires and toward students' interests and desires. When this occurs, it's a game changer for all!

CHAPTER 1

Rethinking Education

In a world of change, the learners shall inherit the earth, while the learned shall find themselves perfectly suited for a world that no longer exists.

—Eric Hoffer, American philosopher

A common narrative surrounding K–12 education goes something like this: when children reach age five, they're ready to enter the system. Elementary teachers teach them to read, write, compute, and listen to prepare them for the next level.

In middle school, there's no more recess or crying over spilled milk. The test score slump that often occurs between fifth and sixth grades leaves little time for slacking off. An ever-changing bell schedule integrates core subjects, electives, and advisement. Signs around campus implore students to work hard, behave, and remember that high school is just around the corner. Despite racing emotions, teachers do their best to keep these preteens focused.

Once in high school, it's full steam ahead. Students hear from a young age that studying hard and getting good grades are their golden tickets to a bright future. If students are put in the right classes with the right teachers, they'll do well. If they graduate with honors, they'll be accepted to the best universities. Once students finish college, a well-paying job awaits. Not only does society prosper, students' quality of life soars too.

Less capable learners land in average or low-level courses where they can meet graduation requirements without a lot of fuss. Some fall behind and transfer to the continuation high school. Others drop out. For those who do graduate, many go directly from high school into lower-paying jobs. Others pursue technical degrees that provide access to higher-skilled occupations.

The story many members of the public believe about education assumes the current system is sound. After all, the majority of us succeeded in this very system and are doing well today. For students who don't do well, we assume we simply need to raise the standards, increase accountability, or provide more resources. However, this false narrative can be deceptive. In theory, education is supposed to pave the path to every youth's future. But, Sir Ken Robinson (2015) has called this a "dangerous myth" that ignores

> the alarming rates of nongraduation from schools and colleges, the levels of stress and depression . . . among students and their teachers, the falling value of a university degree, the rocketing costs of getting one, and the rising levels of unemployment among graduates and nongraduates alike. (p. xxii)

This inaccurate line of thought can also undermine many well-intentioned reforms that set out to improve the system.

Our job, as educators and administrators, is to provide a sense of perspective and context for the way we prepare students. Simply hoping change won't happen or tying our wagons to outdated practices won't cut it. The K–12 education system is of this world, not separate from it (Marx, 2014). Every institution in society is facing a reset. No one, not even our most beloved teachers and administrators, gets a free pass on this journey of rethinking the purpose of education.

This chapter lays the foundation for this book by discussing the shifting paradigm of schooling in a world that is experiencing technological, social, and economic changes at record pace. It makes the case for elevating students beyond average as we prepare them to enter an "any-collar" workforce. It will then delve into the characteristics required for future-ready teaching and learning, including the need for constructive rebellion against conformity. The chapter concludes with Points to Ponder and Rapid-Fire Ideas to get your team started on its journey to reimagine education in a world where learning is available anytime, anywhere, and at any speed.

The Changing Paradigm of Schooling

According to the PDK Poll of the Public's Attitudes Toward the Public Schools, Americans overwhelmingly want schools to do more than educate students in the core subjects (Phi Delta Kappan, 2017). In fact, when judging school quality, the public gives more weight to students' job preparation and interpersonal development than to test scores. While they still value traditional preparation, the vast majority of Americans (82 percent) wants to see career-related course offerings, even if it means students will spend less time in academic classes. And 86 percent believe the schools in their community should offer certificate programs that qualify students for employment in a field that doesn't call for a four-year degree (Phi Delta Kappan, 2017).

If we want students to be prepared for whatever awaits them, our paradigm of *schooling* must change. One important change should be to the unrestrained focus on college entrance requirements. Algebra serves as a perfect case in point. Despite only 5 percent of entry-level jobs in the U.S. calling for proficiency in algebra, passing algebra remains a high school graduation requirement in most states (Rubin, 2016). If students want to work for NASA, they should be proficient mathematicians. But plumbers, playwrights, and pediatricians need other key competencies. Making algebra a mandatory graduation requirement overemphasizes a skill that's not vital for the majority of the workforce. Even worse, it widens the opportunity gap for thousands of students who can't pass algebra and subsequently leave high school without a diploma.

Another K–12 paradigm that calls for rethinking is the "college for all" philosophy that has come to dominate American culture (Fleming, 2016). Across the nation, we find policies and practices that encourage students to pursue a four-year degree over any other path. Meanwhile, student loan debt has closed in on $1.6 trillion, representing the second-highest consumer debt in America behind home mortgages (Goldy-Brown, 2019).

With 66 percent of students enrolling in a four-year university directly out of high school, young people *are* pursuing their dreams of higher earnings. However, many are discovering the job market and their subsequent earning power aren't commensurate with the degrees they hold. *Middle skills jobs*, which require education beyond high school but less than a four-year degree, actually make up the largest part of the labor market in all fifty states (Fleming, 2016). Not only are these jobs in high demand, they offer good salaries and income mobility. Nonetheless, employees are struggling to find enough trained workers in occupations like law enforcement, energy operations, aviation, and the construction and manufacturing trades. Unfortunately, educators, parents, state and federal policymakers, and the media perpetuate this misalignment by encouraging students to attend any university and major in anything under the pretext that there's only one way to achieve job security, social mobility, and financial prosperity (Fleming, 2016).

PERSPECTIVES FROM THE FIELD

As students, we have no say on what we learn or how we learn it. Yet, we're expected to absorb it all, take it all in, and be able to run the world someday. We're expected to raise our hands to use the restroom, then three months later be ready to go to college or have a full-time job, support ourselves, and live on our own. It's not logical.

—Kate Simonds (2015), age 17, TEDx video "I'm 17"

In classrooms today it is evident that some practices have shifted on the surface, although the basic foundation of industrial-era schooling remains in place. Teachers now list assignments on a whiteboard instead of a chalkboard; they share content via document cameras instead of overhead projectors; they arrange desks in table groupings instead of rows. Chromebooks are now present and available for student use, but sit on carts waiting to be checked out. While instructional methods include "talk and turns," group activities, and looking up information on the internet, most academic work remains teacher directed. Unless schools serve current students differently than they served previous generations, students will be confined to learning things because they have to, not because they want to or can.

Vital Skills for a Changing Economy

Social media manager, *app designer*, *offshore wind farmer*, and *drone photographer* are all jobs that didn't exist prior to 2010. Today, these occupations are on the rise. Since job requirements change on a dime, the skills students need to secure a job aren't necessarily the same skills they'll need to keep that job. As such, employers are calling on schools to equip learners with skills and dispositions that can transfer to any line of work.

While a variety of frameworks describe the 21st century skills vital for success, seven themes stand out: (1) collaboration and teamwork; (2) creativity and imagination; (3) agility and adaptability; (4) critical thinking and problem solving; (5) initiative and entrepreneurialism; (6) oral and written communication; and (7) leadership and civic responsibility (Hanover Research, 2011; Wagner, 2008). Employers say the lessons students need for their future are less about reading, writing, and arithmetic, and more about influencing others, figuring things out, and engaging with people across time zones (Friedman & Mandelbaum, 2011). Additionally, these same employers expect new hires to be "creative creators or creative servers"—people who can refine and reinvent tasks as needed (p. 88). It's hard to imagine how a student trained in passive listening can learn to create, collaborate, or think deeply about issues.

Regardless of how we define the vital skills for the 21st century, the 22nd century will be here before we know it. Although general cognitive ability is important, other attributes have moved to the head of the class in the employment arena. Let's consider the hiring practices at Google. Receiving nearly three million job applications each year, Google is twenty-five times more selective than Harvard, Princeton, or Yale (Bock, 2015). However, in 2010, after an in-depth analysis of the company's hiring data, Google ended its practice of using grades, transcripts, and college degrees as screening tools. In an interview with the *New York Times*, then–vice president of people operations Laszlo Bock called academic performance indicators worthless criteria for predicting future job performance (Bryant, 2013). Google finds the best among millions by looking at leadership ability, knowledge of the role, and "Googleyness." Some might confuse Googleyness with culture fit; however, the company is strongly against hiring people who sound and act like everyone else. They want people who are offbeat, willing to challenge the status quo, and bring new perspectives to their team. Interview questions like *Tell us what could go wrong in this situation* or *If you wanted to bring your dog to work but one of your team members was allergic to dogs, what would you do?* help hiring managers determine if a candidate has the mindset to become a "Googler." Academic excellence is just that—academic (Bock, 2015).

Present-day academic curricula assume that students will naturally develop the skills and dispositions employers seek as they matriculate through the school system. But nothing could be further from the truth. Knowledge remains inert unless it's activated with deliberate, purposeful experiences. As educators, though we may not be able to dictate statewide or national curricula, we can still identify which parts of the curriculum are best suited to develop the essential dispositions to ensure these attributes receive the time and attention they deserve. Intentional, integrated professional development helps teachers recognize how to activate these skills inside and outside the classroom. There's no reason teaching and learning have to be so isolated.

A Farewell to Average

Every segment of society is changing quickly. A major driver of this change is the free, always-open internet. New ideas zip across the planet at warp speed, creating an international network of connectedness. Back in 1874, Alexander Graham Bell invented the first telephone. It took seventy-five years for the telephone to reach fifty million users, the coveted mark of a technological revolution (Interactive Schools, 2018). Comparing this with the acceleration of other new technology reveals a trend. The radio reached the fifty million user mark in thirty-eight years. The television— which was initially deemed too expensive to become a popular consumer product— made it into fifty million households in thirteen years (Interactive Schools, 2018). The internet hit fifty million users in four years. Twitter took a mere nine months (Interactive Schools, 2018). Additionally, innovation is no longer confined to think tanks in the Silicon Valley. Twelve-year-olds now write code, build mobile apps, and start their own businesses.

As technology advances, the education necessary to utilize it grows too. In essence, education and technology are in a bit of a race (Fadel, Bialik, & Trilling, 2015). Moreover, the notion of education for employment has moved away from routine, impersonal tasks toward more creative, complex tasks that only humans can perform. It no longer matters if a good idea comes from the top floor, shop floor, or someone's garage. In *That Used to Be Us*, Pulitzer Prize–winning author Thomas Friedman and coauthor Michael Mandelbaum (2011) explain:

> In this hyper-connected world, there is increasingly no "here" and no "there," there is no "in" and no "out," there is only "good," "better," and "best," and managers and

> entrepreneurs everywhere now have greater access than ever to the better and best people, robots, and software everywhere. This makes it more vital than ever that we have schools elevating and inspiring more of our young people into those "better" and "best" categories, because even "good" might not cut it anymore and "average" is definitely over. (p. 106)

Experts say there's never been a worse time for people with "ordinary" skills to be looking for work (Tucker, 2017). This is because computers and automated systems perform "ordinary" tasks at extraordinary speed. The ability to learn new things, adapt to changing environments, and do imaginative work is the gold standard for high-demand, high-wage employment. While *smart* may get an applicant in the door, it won't move him or her past the lobby (Friedman & Mandelbaum, 2011). Students need a sound academic foundation coupled with an ability to see beyond the obvious to recognize emerging trends and patterns, no matter what field or passion they may decide to pursue.

The Any-Collar Workforce

Despite huge employment shifts in the later part of the 20th century, claims that all of America's blue-collar jobs have gone to Mexico or that the majority of white-collar work is being outsourced to India are simply untrue (Paquette, 2017). Also untrue are stories that it's only a matter of time before U.S. workers are replaced by robots. While organizations are increasingly using technology to automate existing processes, the majority are upgrading structures to maximize the value of both humans and machines (Agarwal, Bersin, Lahiri, Schwartz, & Volini, 2018). The goal is to *complement* what people do, not replace them.

As we think about preparing students for the workforce of tomorrow, we need to consider the skills and dispositions that will guarantee a symbiotic relationship among employees, machines, and consumers. Today's workforce is a dynamic ecosystem, where employee-employer relationships are redefined in a variegated labor market (Agarwal et al., 2018). So, let's take a look at the changing skills and dispositions needed for the white-collar, blue-collar, camouflage-collar, and no-collar occupations of the future.

White-Collar Workers

Our doctors, lawyers, engineers, pilots, programmers, bankers, and teachers must be nimble and flexible. In these fields, thinking and learning are constant since information changes so quickly. Rather than spending time looking for more efficient ways to do old work, employers ask their white-collar workers to innovate and invent entirely new ways to do the work (Friedman & Mandelbaum, 2011).

Kaiser, the largest health care system in the U.S., is one of many companies leading the way in reimagining white-collar work. Its coordinated, connected, and convenient patient care model allows people to see their doctor, get an X-ray, have blood drawn, and pick up a prescription all in the same building (Levine, 2017).

When Kaiser opens its first school of medicine in 2020, students will see patients and interact with families in their very first year. One of only a handful of medical schools in America not connected to a university, the California-based provider has also decided to waive tuition for every student in its first five graduating classes. Using a case-based curriculum, medical students will be assigned to study groups and teams of specialists, primary care doctors, nurses, and therapists. In these "integrated clerkships" there is no separation of science and application as students learn it, see it, and practice doing it. Kaiser's goal is to ensure physicians-in-the-making become aggressive champions for their patients in every field of medicine—no matter where they make their careers (Goodnough, 2019).

Blue-Collar Workers

Our machinists, mechanics, production line workers, farmers, miners, and transportation workers must possess a clear understanding of how their jobs add value wherever they are in the company chain. A sense of presence and expertise in human interaction is necessary for blue-collar workers to share their ideas for making a product better. In the latter part of the 20th century, workers in these trades generally performed manual tasks that called for limited knowledge or critical thinking. Today's blue-collar workers, however, are expected to function more like "technical careerists" than cogs on an assembly line where conveyer belts dictate the momentum (Wilke, 2019, p. 3).

One company that has managed to transform its production model is American conglomerate DuPont. Founded in 1802 as a gunpowder mill, DuPont is one of the most sustained industries in the world. With a vast portfolio of products including Nylon, Teflon, Mylar, Lycra, and Kevlar, the company has revamped its employee development programs to reflect changing needs (Ponzo, 2013). In the past, employees learned a set of tasks and repeated those tasks over and over again. Today, engineers and line operators work side by side to solve problems, improve production time, and make decisions together. Systemwide operations software allows employees at any plant to suggest ways to enhance equipment, boost manufacturing processes, and improve technology. The idea is for every employee to add value, no matter where they fall in the company chain. DuPont's determination to address the blue-collar image gap is reflected in the time leaders spend creating an environment where everyone brings their best thinking to work (Ponzo, 2013).

Camouflage-Collar Workers

Engagements in Afghanistan, Iraq, and other remote parts of the world have required new training for our military. During the 20th century, the primary mission of the U.S. armed forces was to deter aggression and re-establish order in a particular region. However, the threats America faces today are decentralized, networked, and syndicated (Friedman & Mandelbaum, 2011). The enemy is no longer a specific country. Instead, some of the greatest hostility comes from loosely-coupled ideologies spread across continents. To that end, our camouflage-collars need a wide range of capabilities, including the ability to adapt to the ever-changing technology that opponents use.

Students who join the military will need to visualize, understand, and decide without necessarily waiting for base commanders to convey every order. In many situations, officers and enlisted personnel respond to unpredictable encounters as they unfold. Every branch of the service is seeking people who understand the complex nature of the environments in which they work along with the courage to offer respectful and candid feedback to superiors (Erdmann, 2013).

Another distinction for the camouflage-collar workforce is the expanding role troops now play in post-conflict stabilization campaigns. Described as *soft power* tasks, deployed personnel—including our National Guard and reservists—need a different skill set to win a war than they need to keep the peace. Reflections on post-conflict operations in Haiti, Somalia, and the Middle East have placed greater emphasis on cultural and political awareness. Military-backed reconstruction efforts require strong interagency collaboration, cohesion in setting priorities, sophisticated leadership, and a well-coordinated ground game (Chong, 2015).

No-Collar Workers

No-collar workers can do anything anyone wants, anytime, anywhere, at any pace. Speechwriters, software developers, web designers, marketing specialists, and Uber drivers build networks through experience, contacts, and a personal brand. They're able to start work at midnight, noon, or after dropping the kids at school. In the United States, 40 percent of the workforce is currently employed in "alternative work arrangements" (Agarwal et al., 2018). Globally this number has surpassed 77 million, with collective earnings exceeding one trillion dollars (Pofeldt, 2016). Many CEOs tell their teams, "I don't care where the work gets done or who does it, just get it done."

An ever-evolving job market makes it hard to gauge what type of workers will be necessary twenty years from now or how to strategically manage these workers. Moreover, students are entering an economy where temporary and short-term engagements have become the norm (Agarwal et al., 2018). As a general rule, education for employment must move away from routine, impersonal tasks to more personal, creative tasks that only people can do well. For graduates to function well in this "any collar" environment, they'll need more than glowing test scores and impressive GPAs. No matter what industry or profession students pursue, our responsibility as educators is to ensure they're ready.

Future-Ready Teaching and Learning

Effective 21st century teaching and learning must reflect what's happening technologically, socially, economically, and globally. When education lags behind other advancements, students are unprepared for the world ahead. Additionally, inequality grows among the population, as the "haves" secure better employment opportunities while the "have-nots" hold little hope of improving their status or circumstances. As a result, both individuals and society suffer in the form of unemployment, underemployment, income gaps, personal stress, and social unrest (Fadel et al., 2015).

 PERSPECTIVES FROM THE FIELD

"We can't educate today's students for tomorrow's world with yesterday's schools."

—Damian LaCroix, Wisconsin superintendent (Marx, 2014, p. 4)

As we consider the values of schooling that are both universally sustainable and forward focused, educators find themselves responding to the push and pull of current constraints and the desire for a better system. For example, traditional accountability measures emphasize effects, not causes, of the heroic work of teachers and administrators (Reeves & DuFour, 2018). This is a *push*. At the same time, teachers and administrators know it's possible for reading scores to improve with a thoughtful multidisciplinary approach to literacy that stimulates lifelong learning. This is a *pull*. Being aware of the competing forces that contribute to our own values will enable us to act as intentional change agents.

Educators are working harder and longer, and producing more than ever before, leading to important questions and choices. But how can we ensure our instruction takes into account economic drivers, social progress indicators, and the overall well-being of students? What should students be learning in the age of robotics, artificial intelligence, and hyperconnectivity? Should we situate the goals of education at the classroom level, the district level, the state level, the national level, or somewhere in between?

The Center for Curriculum Redesign (Fadel et al., 2015) has laid out the ideal case for future-focused teaching and learning through its four-dimensional model of education (see figure 1.1, page 14). The first dimension—*knowledge*—includes traditional subjects like mathematics, reading, and language arts, along with interdisciplinary themes such as STEAM, career and technical education (CTE), global literacy, and entrepreneurialism. The second dimension represents *skills*, including the four Cs—creativity, critical thinking, communication, and collaboration. The third dimension is *character*. Character comprises interpersonal dispositions like mindfulness, curiosity, courage, resilience, ethics, and leadership. The fourth dimension lies outside the overlapping circles, yet remains inside the sphere of education's purpose. Referred to as *meta-learning*, this outer dimension represents the process by which learners become aware of and in control of the habits, perceptions, questions, and growth that propel their own learning. All four dimensions interconnect to establish a framework that takes into account trends, challenges, and future predictions. It also ensures the students we turn loose into the world are the complete package.

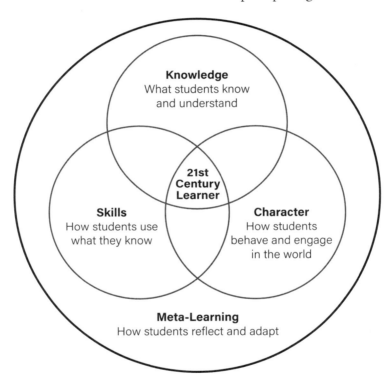

Source: Fadel et al., 2015, p. 32. Used with permission.

Figure 1.1: Four-dimensional model of education.

As the world becomes more interconnected, our efforts must reflect a broader purpose. These efforts can no longer be driven by an either/or proposition (my students are either college bound or they're not; I'm either an academic counselor or a social emotional counselor; I either implement the curriculum with fidelity or ad-lib as I go). The four touchstones in this book provide a framework to incorporate the four dimensions of education into future-ready teaching and learning. By challenging conventional mindsets and structures that hold some learners back, we can refine our curriculum so that every student has the chance to thrive in a global economy.

Constructive Rebellion Against Conformity

Throughout our lives, society pushes us to conform (Gino, 2016). We expect and teach conformity starting in preschool, initially under the guise of safety. In the elementary grades, teachers prompt students to listen, walk quietly down the halls, and follow all the rules. Middle and high schools impose order via a litany of policies and consequences that ensure compliance and teach social convention about public behavior. By the time students enter the workplace, conformity has been so engrained they have no choice but to embrace it.

Rules exist as a means to protect people from the damage others inflict. But the problem with conformity in education is that children aren't born standardized (Robinson, 2015). This leads one to wonder how strict a school really has to be. How many constraints should schools impose on faculty, who are supposed to let creativity flow? And what about the prevailing wisdom that guides administrators to establish processes that follow organizational norms? If students are to advance society and develop products, ventures, and technologies that help everyone, then our system of education has to be less stifling. This includes more deliberate pushback against the conformity creep that consciously or unconsciously permeates a work culture.

As school and district teams strengthen their work together, *constructive rebellion* should be part of the equation. Constructive rebellion encourages people to deviate from the status quo. It gives team members permission to become rebels with the right cause. Nonconformists aren't anarchists. Rather, they're practical change agents who want to cut through red tape to bring better practices to bear (Gino, 2016).

Table 1.1 illustrates the distinctions between constructive and destructive rebellion. Strategies to foster constructive rebellion in schools include defining what teachers need to do, rather than how they do it; asking for proof; insisting team members (not the principal) come up with solutions; and supporting experimentation. When schools allow (and encourage) team members to express their authentic selves at work, they become more committed to the organization and its purpose.

Table 1.1: Constructive Versus Destructive Rebellion

Constructive Rebels	Destructive Rebels
Create	Complain
Ask questions	Make assertions
Display optimism	Display pessimism
Generate energy	Zap energy
Pinpoint causes	Point fingers
Focus on the mission	Focus on themselves
Attract	Alienate
Show passion	Show anger

Source: Adapted from Kelly & Medina, 2015, p. 2.

PERSPECTIVES FROM THE FIELD

Decades' worth of psychological research has shown that we feel accepted and believe that our views are more credible when our colleagues share them. But although conformity may make us feel good, it doesn't let us reap the benefits of authenticity.

—Francesca Gino, professor and researcher, Harvard University (Gino, 2016, p. 6)

Many educators find it hard to resist pressure from colleagues and are reluctant to say uncomfortable things. But, without the insight and perspective to know when to push back, teachers and administrators will struggle to remain relevant. Companies like BlackBerry, Polaroid, and MySpace once had winning formulas too (Gino, 2016). We saw what happened when these movers and shakers failed to update their strategies until it was too late. Schools are no different. Rethinking the purpose of education gives us a reason to stay engaged.

Educators talk a lot, but what are we actually saying? Without challenging existing practices by asking "why" and "what if" questions, it's hard to change mindsets or create energy around getting better. Blending conformity with nonconformity requires a delicate balance. On the one hand, we don't want a lack of conformity to send the message that doing our own thing or working in isolation is good for students. On the other hand, rigid and inflexible practices limit our ability to come up with new ideas and achieve shared goals. Everyone needs variety and challenge in their jobs to perform well; without it, we switch to autopilot. Constructive rebellion is a way to shake things up in schools without finger pointing, complaining, or alienating peers.

Conclusion: There Is No Limit for Better

Education for employment calls upon schools to move away from century-old routines to cultivate the vast diversity of young people's talents and aspirations. Educators must give equal weight to the vital skills and habits that will close the widening gap between what's being taught in schools and what the economy actually needs. Most jobs today demand a different skill set than that necessary for the jobs that have vanished. This has caught many educators off guard. Nevertheless, we can no longer turn a blind eye to economic realities and our responsibilities as educators to do something about it.

Communities across America depend on a range of talent, roles, and occupations to remain vibrant. Sir Ken Robinson (2015) points out, "The work of electricians, builders, plumbers, chefs, paramedics, carpenters, mechanics, engineers, security staff, and all the rest (who may or may not have college degrees) is absolutely vital to the quality of each of our lives" (p. 17). Many people in these occupations find their careers fulfilling and financially rewarding. To secure rewarding careers, students need exposure to the variegated paths available in the "any collar" marketplace. There is no fixed utopia for education (Robinson, 2015). At the same time, there is no limit for getting better. Although teaching is a highly individualized endeavor, the issues surrounding teaching are increasingly global. Healthy schools are interdependent learning organizations that aren't afraid to disrupt the status quo to improve.

The following chapter lays the groundwork to embrace a culture of innovation as a gateway for getting better. The emphasis in chapter 2 is to examine the drivers of innovative thinking and how to put this thinking into practice. Readers will learn how the best companies and the best schools use innovation as a centerpiece for new ideas that everyone can get behind.

Touchstone Takeaways

Consider the following Points to Ponder and Rapid-Fire Ideas on your own or within a teacher or leadership team to cultivate a broader vision of future-focused teaching and learning.

Points to Ponder

1. Would you want to be a student in your own classroom today? Why or why not?

2. How might you align staff or team meetings to rethink education? What paradigms of schooling need to change in your building or district?

3. College professor Kevin Fleming (2016) argues that we should broaden the "college for all" rhetoric dominating the K–12 system to a mantra of a "post-high school credential for all" (p. 9). Which philosophy permeates your organization? What interplay between academics and application is in place now in your school or district?

4. Using the Four-Dimensional Model of Education in figure 1.1 (page 14), what immediate shifts in teaching and learning might lead to longer-term change?

5. How might you embrace constructive rebellion to move conversations forward? What nonjudgmental language will you use to address practices that inadvertently hinder future-ready learning?

Rapid-Fire Ideas

Consider the following rapid-fire ideas as you begin implementing the ideas from this chapter in your classroom.

Consider Success in the New Economy

Watch Kevin Fleming's "Success in the New Economy" video at your next team meeting (www.youtube.com/watch?v=zs6nQpVI164). Share takeaways. Discuss how the team can create upstream changes to shore up students' paths to the future.

Empower the Collar

Future occupations will consist of many shapes, sizes, and colors. But, a common thread in this "any collar" environment is a worker's ability to look at a task and see the desired outcome. At the same time, employers expect workers to imagine different ways to achieve the outcome. Create a graphic organizer that depicts how you empower students to recognize desired outcomes and imagine different ways to accomplish tasks.

Evaluate Your School's Readiness

Individually or in a team, complete the worksheet in figure 1.2. Discuss your responses to track current progress as it relates to preparing students for a fast-changing world. Determine a good starting point to develop a shared vision for undertaking this work.

Directions: Complete this quiz to examine the thinking, behaviors, and systems in place in your school or district as they relate to preparing students for the future that awaits them.

	Not in Place 0	Emerging 1	Progressing 2	We're There 3
1. My school or district maintains a clear vision for developing well-educated, employable students.				
2. Staff members believe school should be done differently than when they were in school.				
3. Teachers understand their role in preparing future-ready learners in spite of the grade level, subject, or content they teach.				
4. My school or district cultivates the vast diversity of students' talents and aspirations across classrooms and disciplines.				
5. My school or district provides students high-leverage experiences that aren't measured on standardized tests.				
6. The culture in my school or district supports nonlinear changes in college and career readiness approaches.				
7. My school or district views everyone (including students) as a leader and learner.				
8. My school or district appreciates where stakeholders (parents, business, community at large) are coming from in their expectations of schools.				
9. In my school or district, trends and future predictions drive shifts in teaching and learning.				
10. My school or district sees constructive rebellion as a way to develop the kind of workforce America is seeking.				

Scoring: Add up the total points for each question. Use the results to begin conversations with peers, administrators, and teams.

25–30: Your school or district is ready to plunge deeper into the concepts and competencies that set students on course to become all the public expects them to be. Existing practices include connections between education and employment.

20–24: Your school or district has some practices and systems in place to address future-ready learning. Team members are poised to identify a starting point for further development.

15–19: Your school or district lacks a shared vision of what a future-ready learner looks like and how to go about getting him or her there. Universal agreement surrounding the why of this work is necessary to make the what of the work more impactful.

Below 15: Your school or district needs a broader understanding of the new paradigm for schooling. A disconnect exists between the role educators in your building or district believe they should play in preparing future-ready learners and the role mainstream society believes they should play.

Figure 1.2: Ground floor quiz—Ready or not?

CHAPTER 2

Implementing Innovative Practices

It is not enough to be busy. So are the ants. The question is: What are we busy about?

—Henry David Thoreau

When I began teaching in the early 1980s, I sifted through the curriculum on my own and taught what seemed important. There were no grade-level standards, no scope and sequence charts, no state tests that counted for anything, and no common planning time. Curriculum was bundled around frameworks that identified a discrete set of skills for each subject area. Teaching was generally an individual endeavor. For the most part, education remained outside the public eye.

To make things more interesting, I made up my own worksheets and crafted special projects to keep students engaged. Students wrote study guides, solved problems of the day, and gave oral reports. I taught subjects in fifty-minute increments sandwiched between morning recess, lunch, and afternoon break. My reading, mathematics, and gifted groups were organized by ability. Textbooks served as the core resource for instruction and classroom activities.

When technology began to make its way into schools, our principal asked teachers to add computer science to the curriculum. At the time, we had a lab of Apple IIe computers and one Commodore 64 per classroom. With the looming opportunity for students to interact with a multimedia universe, I was determined to ensure my students were ready.

The third-grade team pooled our best thinking to design a three-week computer science unit. After a few hours of planning, we felt we had strong lessons that would make our principal proud. Students would learn what a computer did (even though we didn't really know ourselves), label all the hardware, and understand the differences among a central processing unit (CPU), monitor, keyboard, and floppy disk. An end-of-unit exam would help us assess what our students had learned. To tie everything together, we invited students to make a computer diorama as an at-home project.

At open house, the students prominently displayed the dioramas around our classroom. I have vivid memories of one dad asking if students ever got to use the computer. I proudly responded, "Why, yes. Every week students get thirty minutes in the computer lab. And for students who finish their work early, they're able to use the classroom computer." His next question stopped me in my tracks: "What's the purpose of my son learning about the parts of the computer without really using the computer?" Of course, there was no good answer. Sadly, I had mistaken the technology surge as a learning outcome rather than a learning tool. Little thought had gone into what students should be able to do with the technology. In fact, the hype of having a shiny new object in my classroom led me to assume students would be motivated by this new object too. By neglecting my own professional development about how this tool might accelerate learning, valuable instructional time became a wasted opportunity. I wonder how many of my former students are roaming the halls of the Silicon Valley telling coworkers what they didn't learn in third grade.

If the goal is to make learning more impactful, we must revolutionize the student experience in innovative ways—otherwise instruction will remain more about us and less about them. Fluid thinking pushes us to tackle common instructional challenges differently than we handled them in the past. With standards, content, technology, and testing forever changing, educators have to rely on *next* practices rather than *best* practices. *Best* practices are about what we do today. *Next* practices are a playbook for tomorrow. Standing in front of a whiteboard lecturing is not a *next* practice.

While the term *innovation* may have become a bit overused, it continues to encapsulate exciting possibilities within our profession. Work is more magical when we design the physical and mental space to experiment with novel ideas. Innovative educators explore new topics with colleagues, and share what they know. They recast instructional strategies to fit the changing times.

This chapter focuses on the first touchstone for future-ready learning: implementing innovative practices (see figure I.1, page 2). These *next* practices derive from a sense of selflessness, risk taking, time, flexibility, and trust. Within this chapter, readers will discover six characteristics of innovative educators and eight themes that underscore how teachers can innovate in their classrooms in an easy way. The chapter also offers tips and tactics to help practitioners make room for innovation within the confines of the school day and academic year. As mentioned earlier in the book, readers should not view these strategies as a prescriptive formula to get from point A to point B. Rather, the strategies can be mixed, matched, and applied as needed, depending on where their schools or classrooms currently fall on the innovation spectrum. The chapter concludes with Points to Ponder and Rapid-Fire Ideas to kickstart educators on their journey to implementing innovative practices.

PERSPECTIVES FROM THE FIELD

Teaching disruptively is about reaching students in new ways . . . then turning them loose on the world.

—Terry Heick (2018), founder and director, TeachThought

Six Characteristics of Innovative Educators

Innovation hasn't always been a hot topic in schools. Nowhere in teacher preparation courses or professional development days do we hear much talk about innovative practices. In fact, we as teachers work hard to eliminate uncertainty through step-by-step lesson plans and prescriptive learning experiences. We go to great lengths to identify objectives, use direct instruction to teach these objectives, and define problems we want students to solve. Adding to the concern is how our principal or supervisor will judge our performance. *Winging it*—as some might think of innovation—is a scary proposition.

Although the conditions in schools aren't ideal for innovation, there are plenty of educators working hard to mix things up. Before we can ask students to be curious, creative learners, we have to understand the context for this work. The biggest question is where to begin—with ourselves, with our students, or somewhere in between?

Whether we are in search of better approaches to use with struggling learners, trying to improve our school's results, or looking for ways to ease the worries of an anxiety-ridden student, new processes are necessary to solve age-old problems. Although we all deal with the same testing requirements, budget constraints, and demographic challenges, there are six characteristics that innovative educators have in common (Couros, 2015; Miller, Latham, & Cahill, 2017).

1. **Innovative educators are problem finders.** Rather than wait for a good problem to surface, innovative educators actively search for problems. They're just as fascinated with figuring things out as their students are. They ask "why" not to be difficult, but to start a ripple effect that leads to applied innovation.

2. **Innovative educators issue grand challenges.** *Grand challenges* are difficult—but important—local, regional, or global events that require unorthodox solutions. From climate change to homelessness, clean water, cyber security, school safety, or aging infrastructure, there is no shortage of grand challenges out there. The aim of a grand challenge is to connect learning outcomes to content and grade-level standards.

3. **Innovative educators borrow freely.** Breakthrough thinking often resides in people with experiences that differ from our own. It occurs when we leave our familiar box to explore less-conventional alternatives. Innovative

educators look outside education for ideas. They borrow freely from imaginative industries to challenge the status quo.

4. **Innovative educators embrace messiness.** Chasing perfection is not part of an innovator's mindset. Innovative educators welcome a sense of *not-yetness*—when things aren't fully under control—by paying heed to the fact that learning and doing are messy.

5. **Innovative educators use technology correctly.** Innovative educators embrace a coherent approach to technology integration that generates relevant insights. Digitally rich learning comes from using the right technology, at the right time, in the right dosage.

6. **Innovative educators are comfortable with mistakes.** Innovative educators push the boundaries of teaching by taking risks. Along with risks come mistakes—mistakes with lessons, mistakes with technology, mistakes with timing, mistakes that students make. When teachers make mistakes, they get back up, dust themselves off, decide what went wrong, and have another go at it.

The formula to bring innovative practices into the classroom is actually not formulaic (Couros, 2015). Instead, it's a combination of methodology, structure, work practices, and ad-libbing. Words like *teaching lean*, *bottom up*, and *participatory* underscore the experience. To avoid innovation limbo, any creative undertaking has to be student-centric and accessible to all.

Eight Themes of Practical DREAMING

By and large, teachers are better executors than innovators. From personal observations and decades working with, supervising, and teaching teachers, I have found that most succeed by sticking with what's already in place rather than trying something new. With little time to analyze and reflect on professional practice, it's easier to repeat what learning *has been* instead of focus on what learning *could be*. Moreover, the majority of teachers is conditioned to teach students from their own worldview and life experiences. Classroom practices tend to conform to a teacher's personal beliefs, opinions, and biases.

Within that framework, *innovation* is an ambiguous term. It can feel like a race with no defined finish line. Hesitation exists among some educators who worry that a less conventional approach won't work in their classrooms. One California teacher described her own skepticism this way:

> Sometimes I think education is a circus. We're just contained in this tent and we take it down in the summer and we put it back up every fall. In fifteen years of teaching, it never occurred to me to look outside of the tent . . . . Optimism is not lacking in schools, but it's all reserved for our students . . . . If teachers viewed themselves as designers and believed they could affect [sic] change, and

really believed in themselves, I think a much better system
is possible. (IDEO, 2013)

Clearly, our mindset about the best way to design and deliver content is essential to any innovative process. In his 2011 State of the Union address, President Obama reminded the nation that thirty years before no one predicted something called "the Internet" would lead to an economic revolution. The President noted that while the future is ours to win, we cannot stand still to get there. To compete for the jobs and industries of the era, America has to "out-innovate, out-educate, and out-build the rest of the world" (Obama, 2011, p. 4). So what will give teachers the confidence and permission they need to "out-educate" the rest of the world? And how do we create more fluid learning environments in order for students to become the innovators and entrepreneurs the nation expects?

I would like to present eight themes that underscore high-imagination learning environments that set us on a path to "out-educate' the rest of the world. Educators who adopt these strategies actualize innovation through practical DREAMING (see the following acronym). Practical dreamers resist the lure of appearances to convert aspirations into reality. They envision a better future for students and take practical steps to get there.

To encourage innovation in classrooms, practical dreamers:

1. **Discover**—Practical dreamers look through multiple lenses to provide a deeper sense of what learners want, need, and deserve. They pursue opportunities to refine instructional approaches beyond the world of education. Practical dreamers pay attention to random events that lead to interesting results. A key question for the Discover theme is, *Do I have imaginative, yet actionable, insights that translate into winning propositions for students?*

2. **Reach**—Practical dreamers quantify their compelling vision of classroom innovation with a set of clear goals and metrics. They view innovation as a critical process for student growth. A key question for the Reach theme is, *Do I have a compelling vision, clear goals, and reachable targets that are substantial enough for me to act without being over the top?*

3. **Explore**—Practical dreamers distinguish worthy ideas from flavor-of-the-month pursuits. They study shifts in pedagogy to separate inconsequential changes from changes that revolutionize learning. A key question for the Explore theme is, *Do I pursue opportunities and technology tools with high value that promote experimentation?*

4. **Accelerate**—Practical dreamers eliminate barriers between a great idea and the end user (students). They test their ideas to ensure they reap the intended outcomes. A key question for the Accelerate theme is, *Do I launch new ideas through fast implementation and assessment without throwing the baby out with the bathwater?*

5. **Mobilize**—Practical dreamers infuse engagement and collaboration throughout the school day—not just during "innovation" time. Their

classroom structures allow ideas to flow freely. Their students see themselves as leaders of innovation too. Key questions for the Mobilize theme are, *Do I foster a learning environment where ideas flow freely, no matter if they come from my students or me? Do students have the knowledge and resources to contribute?*

6. **Inventory**—Practical dreamers select activities and assignments through discerning choices, even when something is too new to know if it's worth the effort. They weed out low-yield activities in favor of high-yield experiences. A key question for the Inventory theme is, *Do I conduct ongoing reviews of activities and assignments and determine the value of these activities and assignments for optimal effect?*

7. **Network**—Practical dreamers use vertical and horizontal networks to connect to thought partners within their own schools, districts, and regions. They pursue experts outside the field of education as valuable contacts and inspiration. A key question for the Network theme is, *Do I strategically engage with a variety of practitioners and partners to pursue novel perspectives and new learning?*

8. **Gauge**—Practical dreamers test new concepts against the capacity and infrastructure necessary to sustain them. They ensure that both teachers and students have a chance to react to a concept before getting too far down the road. A key question for the Gauge theme is, *Do I conceive and test concepts at the right time, at the right magnitude, with the right intentions?*

Consider the type of innovator you are now. Are you *visionary*—someone who sees a shift coming before anyone else? Or are you more *strategic*—someone who carefully plans innovation around a specific purpose to gain an advantage? Perhaps you're a *fast follower*. Fast followers may not come up with an idea, but they get on board quickly to out-deliver innovation over others. Or are you a *disruptor*? Disruptors don't wait for new technology or new approaches to find them. Disruptive innovators, and others like them, are always looking for the next thing that will radically change their work. However you define yourself as an innovator, your actions should align with your goals. Practical DREAMING boosts job performance and brings out the inner innovator in you.

Having introduced the characteristics of innovative educators and the mindset necessary to dream big, this chapter now moves on to strategies educators can use to implement innovative practices in their schools and classrooms.

Strategies to Increase Innovation in the Student Environment

The following sections introduce several strategies readers can use to increase innovation in their schools and classrooms. The strategies include:

- A Lesson in Subtraction
- Habits of Mind That Make Schools Shine
- Hot Teams and the Design Thinking Framework
- The Stickiness Factor

A Lesson in Subtraction

All educators have an interest in improving student learning. Coming up with new ideas is invigorating. But trying to synthesize an avalanche of new ideas without first letting go of old ideas can cause a brain drain. As schools layer new initiatives on top of old traditions, it leaves little room for the *best* elements to shine. We hear colleagues talk about *initiative fatigue, overload,* and *burnout*. The tendency to launch more changes than any staff member can reasonably handle is akin to education malpractice. Emotional responses to mandated changes are thus rarely positive.

Conventional wisdom holds that schools are starving from a shortage of good ideas. In reality, many schools are suffering from a bad case of indigestion. Schools tend to implement new initiatives in a fragmented, haphazard manner. Sadly, most new initiatives have a disappointing track record. It takes time for teachers to develop familiarity and a certain level of comfort with untried strategies. With each new initiative, the time and energy to implement it diminish. Initiative fatigue sets in, leading to resistance and apathy.

Teachers often view innovative teaching as another initiative. Asking teachers to do more creative things without focus and direction leads to confusion and overload. But innovation isn't about putting every shiny new object into the curriculum. It's about identifying objects—both shiny and dull—to leave *out*. In this age of abundance, those who get ahead in life are those who practice the art of omission. To contemplate the benefits of a new idea—perhaps implementing project-based learning or adopting a new online learning management system—we must first consider the impact and consequences it has for teachers. In essence, to what degree do people see the innovation as better than the program it's replacing? And how compatible is the innovation with the values, experiences, and needs of potential adopters?

The Initiative Inventory in figure 2.1 (page 28) is a high-leverage activity—an activity that maximizes efficiency and effectiveness—to help teachers and administrators discern how current innovations and initiatives affect practice. The idea is to objectively examine what's already in place without favoring or opposing one initiative over another. Teams can use the Inventory to decide if a program is truly impacting student outcomes or simply keeping everyone busy. Absent tangible results, an innovation or initiative is unlikely to be powerful enough to make a difference.

Once staff members have completed the Initiative Inventory and compared individual rankings, a facilitator can lead the entire group in a conversation about the overall findings. Specifically, the facilitator should have each group share any initiatives they feel should be eliminated or reimaged. For example, if a group believes

Part I: Work in teams to identify the "top ten" initiatives or programs in your district or school plan. Once the list is complete, indicate if this initiative or program is district-initiated (DI), district-endorsed (DE), or site-led (SL). Use the following definitions to help you decide.

- District-initiated (DI)—This initiative is in every school and implemented with the same degree of regularity from site to site (for example, English in a Flash, Raz-Kids, common assessments).
- District-endorsed (DE)—This initiative is in most schools, but varies in its degree of implementation (for example, STEAM, career pathways, dual language program).
- Site-led (SL)—This initiative is unique to the site with discretion of the principal or staff to implement as they see fit (for example, AVID, International Baccalaureate).

Part II: Use the following questions to evaluate the quality and effectiveness of each initiative. Discuss the evidence used for your evaluation. Put an X in the appropriate column to indicate if this initiative or program should be Kept As Is, Reimagined, or Eliminated. Jot down your ideas, impediments, and questions in the space provided.

- Does this initiative or program lead to high-quality learning aligned with the vision?
- Does this initiative or program have measurable evidence that ensures students of all ability levels are well equipped to meet the challenges of education, work, and life?
- Is this initiative or program supported by a priority goal in the district's strategic plan?
- Do the outcomes from this initiative or program justify the time and resources required to support it?
- Should this initiative or program be kept as is, reimagined, or eliminated?

Part III: Share your results with other teams. Reach consensus as a staff or department about programs or services that should be reimagined or eliminated.

"Top Ten" Initiatives or Programs Underway This Year in Your School or District	District-Initiated (DI), District-Endorsed (DE), or Site-Led (SL)		Keep As Is	Reimagine	Eliminate	Ideas, Impediments, Questions
1.						
2.						
3.						
4.						
5.						
6.						
7.						
8.						
9.						
10.						

Figure 2.1: Initiative inventory.

*Visit **go.SolutionTree.com/21stcenturyskills** for a free reproducible version of this figure.*

the STEM program should be "reimagined," it's important to drill down into the specific parts of the program that are and aren't working. If common assessments emerge as something to "eliminate," these concerns merit attention. A frank discussion about the amount of testing going on in a building can lead to a more coherent approach to assessment.

The purpose of the inventory is to guide a team's review of current initiatives so that a clearer picture of effective strategies and committed resources emerges. By examining the full range of initiatives underway in a school, teachers, principals, and central office leaders gain a better perspective of how overload hinders innovation. The point isn't to replace every eliminated program with something new. Rather, the point is to practice subtraction in schools as fervently as we practice addition.

Habits of Mind That Make Schools Shine

Schools can't become leading innovators without an innovative culture. However, establishing this culture isn't as simple as following a given set of steps that move people from point A to point B. I have identified seven habits of mind that fuel innovative cultures.

1. **Shared purpose:** The degree to which people embrace the same goals and values to move the organization forward

2. **Energy:** The degree to which people feel challenged and excited about their work

3. **Influence:** The degree to which people feel they can make an impact

4. **Reciprocity:** The degree to which people exchange ideas, learn together, and give one another other similar advantages

5. **Spontaneity:** The degree to which people act on their impulses or go with the flow

6. **Risk taking:** The degree to which people try new things and push themselves to increase their competence or skills

7. **Accountability:** The degree to which people feel responsible for and own the outcomes

Across North America, schools are working hard to reinvent education. But how do they create a culture of innovation that people want to be a part of and imitate? How do these habits of mind parlay into meaningful experiences for learners? One shining example is Wiseburn–Da Vinci High School (www.davincischools.org), located one mile south of the Los Angeles International Airport. Previously a K–8 school district, Wiseburn Unified has partnered with the Da Vinci charter school to transform the former home of Douglas Aircraft into a magnificent new high school. The site was purchased by the school district in 2015 and completely rebuilt to house three independent charter high schools: Da Vinci Communications, Da Vinci Design, and Da Vinci Science. Each school occupies its own floor of the 210,000-square-foot facility. Community members, school leaders, teachers, and architects collaborated on the building design to create a modern environment that humanizes the student experience, reflecting a desire for learning that is socially based and untethered.

When you enter the campus, the physical environment speaks volumes about what matters there. Four courageous commitments—displayed throughout the building—exemplify the beliefs that are protected and promoted among Wiseburn–Da Vinci teachers and students.

1. Stay engaged.
2. Speak your truth.
3. Experience discomfort (embrace the struggle).
4. Accept non-closure.

The lack of clutter throughout the building is also striking. Technology is present, but subtle; people use it for a purpose. Neighborhood pods open up to common areas connected by a four-story atrium. Students spread out wherever they're comfortable, with the freedom and confidence to take ownership of their learning. Teachers hold office hours and one-on-one tutorials. The first floor houses a theater and auditorium, recording studio, and professional development center for practitioners who come from around the globe to study the school's unique model. The innovative physical environment influences how students behave, collaborate, and perform. It's their "third" teacher.

Partners from industry, higher education, and nonprofit organizations support every facet of school life. From Boeing, to Chevron, to UCLA, to the Ahmanson Foundation, there is a commitment from external collaborators to serve students to the very best of their individual and collective ability. For example, students gain work experience in high-skill, high-demand jobs through paid and unpaid internships. Educators facilitate mentoring opportunities with industry experts. Each semester, students complete a presentation of learning (POL) to demonstrate mastery in a formal setting. POLs consist of an oral presentation followed by a question-and-answer segment from a panel of teachers and industry partners. Finally, to create affordable pathways to college, students can enroll in UCLA extension courses two evenings per week. With a desire to build a pipeline from kindergarten to career, the cutting-edge curriculum relies on input from leading experts to ensure real-world application and workforce alignment.

To meet growing demands from educators who want to learn more about the school's design, the Da Vinci Institute offers access to fellowships, resources, and deeper dives into the philosophy that makes the school such an amazing place to work and learn. While education at every level focuses on supporting innovation, the more important trend is that Wiseburn–Da Vinci High School reaches beyond the education sector to do it. New alliances make the school functional, inviting, and able to serve students in ways they want to be served.

Hot Teams and the Design Thinking Framework

Tom Kelley runs the marketing side of IDEO, a leading product design firm. Tom's brother David started the Palo Alto company in 1977, and one of its first big projects was the Apple mouse. Today, IDEO is the world's most celebrated design firm, where brainstorming is a science and work is play. Projects in every shape and size create an environment where employees team, dream, and stream ideas together.

In his bestselling book *The Art of Innovation*, Tom Kelley (2001) contends it's no accident that teams form the heart of an organization's culture. While some companies labor through monthly meetings rehashing the same issues, IDEO relies on *Hot Teams* to accomplish its goals. Hot Teams form around specific projects and disciplines, similar to the way Hollywood film studios assemble teams around a script. The actors, director, set designers, and countless others work together on the storyline until the movie is finished with production.

Hot Teams can range in size from three to twenty, with team members picking their "studio" (that is, the project they want to work on) and their leader. When IDEO gets a new project, it assigns the work to a team that's going to be excited about it. Teams work together for a set period of time, with movement allowed between teams and among studios. Each studio is infused with a clear purpose, loads of passion, and fast deadlines.

Hundreds of cutting-edge products, including the Polaroid camera, PalmPilot, and mechanical whale used in the film *Free Willy*, have come from Hot Teams. To turn out awesome ideas, teams use a combination of creativity and structure to challenge the perceived constraints of a problem. As pioneers of design thinking, IDEO finds out what customers really want and need instead of simply looking at historical data or making guesses.

 PERSPECTIVES FROM THE FIELD

> Good companies and good [leaders] are astute observers of people, teams, technologies, and trends. They see quirks and patterns. What makes IDEO different is that we put a lot of steam and spark behind our observations.
>
> — Tom Kelley (2001), author and partner of IDEO

The leadership of IDEO also founded Stanford University's Institute of Design (known as the "d.school"; https://dschool.stanford.edu), where its original founder, David Kelley, serves as the academic director in the School of Design Engineering. At the d.school, professional development experiences for teachers take place in hotel lobbies, public parks, restaurants, school lunch rooms, and empty storefronts to create an ambiance of immersive learning (Wise, 2017). They use the design thinking framework in figure 2.2 (page 32) as a guide to infuse experimentation with problem solving.

Source: Adapted from d.school, 2010.

Figure 2.2: Design thinking framework.

The d.school's design thinking framework contains five important steps.

1. **Empathize:** First, the team has to understand the audience for whom it's designing. The problems we're trying to solve in schools are rarely our own. To build empathy, we have to observe and talk with users (preferably students) to find out who they are, what's important to them, and what current programs, services, or environments do not currently address. We can learn a lot about someone's thinking, goals, and passions by talking with them where they live, study, or work.

2. **Define:** A well-defined design challenge is clear on the ultimate problem the team hopes to solve or the impact it aspires to have. A single sentence or question should convey your challenge. Distilling a challenge down to a specific user group (for example, English learners, special education students, or at-risk youth) helps the team come up with a variety of ideas and potential solutions.

3. **Ideate:** Ideation goes beyond brainstorming to ensure a team generates an abundance of ideas, including those that seem ridiculous or far-fetched. The best ideation sessions have no agendas and no presentations. People simply come together to talk about what's possible and see if there are any potential projects or prototypes among the ideas. The point is to go for volume and build on others' ideas.

4. **Prototype:** A prototype can be anything that takes a physical form, from a doodle, to a storyboard, to an actual model. The most successful prototypes are living models in which the design team, users, and others can interact. What the team learns from the interactions drives deeper empathy and better solutions.

5. **Test:** Testing is the chance to gain feedback on the team's solutions and refine them to make them better. The test phase is also the place to expect the unexpected as actual users experience the prototype. In this stage, it's essential not to overexplain how the prototype should work. The idea is to let the user do the talking and reacting.

Hot Teams are incubators—places where ideas hatch, relationships blossom, futuristic thinking occurs, and bureaucracy doesn't exist. Potential Hot Team issues in schools might include designing the ideal staff lounge, reimagining classroom space, building an online teacher collaboration tool, hacking the hallways to make passing periods less chaotic, or anything else a team finds to be a challenge. Building teamwork into seemingly ordinary tasks creates a sense of energy and excitement that is contagious. If we want students to think critically and solve real-world problems, the adults who serve them need to model this behavior too. Hot Teams are the perfect vehicle to make this happen.

We all face design challenges at work. Whether these challenges represent a large-scale problem (like increasing student attendance rates) or a small speed bump (like keeping rambunctious students occupied at lunch time), they are real, varied, and complex. They call for new perspectives and new approaches. Thinking like designers allows educators to create a more desirable future together. It also offers a proven process for teachers and administrators to be more intentional about addressing students' wants and needs. At the heart of design thinking is a sense of optimism and user centeredness.

The Stickiness Factor

How is it that a great idea can spread like wildfire in one building and barely catch a spark in another? Figuring out how to make an idea contagious is one of the most difficult aspects of school change. In the popular book *The Tipping Point*, Malcolm Gladwell (2002) calls this the *stickiness factor*. Unless people are touched by what they hear or see, they won't be moved to action. With so many ideas to absorb, a faculty can become sticky-resistant. For a new concept to succeed, the values and commitments of the organization have to sustain it. The tipping point comes as we tinker at the margins (Gladwell, 2002).

One company with an uncanny ability to predict trends and tinker at the margins is Apple. In 2009, CEO Tim Cook (who was chief operating officer at the time) told a group of shareholders:

> We are the most focused company that I know of . . . We say no to great ideas in order to keep the amount of things we focus on very small in number so that we can put enormous energy behind the ones we do choose. (McChesney, Covey, & Huling, 2012, p. 29)

Cook went on to explain that the table they were sitting around could hold every product Apple made despite it being a $40 billion company at the time (McChesney et al., 2012). As competitors produce dozens of phones each year to chase the company's market share, Apple continues to make just one.

Industry analysts have studied the guiding principles that give Apple products their stickiness factor (Bajarin, 2012). As you read the following list, think about the differences we might see for students if we applied these same principles in education.

- **Those who create the products have to want it themselves:** In many companies, engineers make things because they can. At Apple, engineers make things they want to use themselves. Every Apple product is designed with the chief user in mind. Imagine if all the lessons we created, textbooks we adopted, and assessments we gave were things we couldn't live without.

If we aren't wowed by the resources we are using, how can we expect our students to be wowed by them?

- **Products must be easy to use:** While industry design is an important aspect of Apple products, if a product isn't easy to use it is deemed worthless. Anything Apple makes has to be intuitive and simple for a customer to learn. Imagine if ease of use became a mantra in schools. Before installing telepresence or buying more Chromebooks, we need to be sure teachers are comfortable with these tools.

- **Keep things simple:** Consumer research shows that while people like choices, too many choices can lead to indecision. By minimizing the number of products it sells, Apple simplifies the decision-making process for customers. In schools, conventional thinking is that the more exposure students have to lots of things, the smarter they'll be. In reality, this thinking hasn't made students smarter or produced stickier learning.

- **Ensure great service and in-store experiences:** When Apple opened its first store in 2002, many predicted it would be a short-lived affair. Yet, whenever a new Apple store opens, large crowds jockey to be the first inside. Store greeters don't ask, "How can I help you?" Instead, they ask, "What would you like to do today?" Customers show up not only to buy something, but for the experience. As educators, we should go to the heart of students' interests and ask, "What would you like to learn today?" Serving up experiences students' way can make all the difference in the world.

- **Introduce something new only if it's better:** Since losing the PC wars to Microsoft, Apple has remained steadfast in prioritizing what it produces. Any new product is often a re-creation of an existing product. For example, a Korean company released the first MP3 player. Apple simply made the device better with the iPod. The first smartphone was invented by IBM. Apple just made it better with the iPhone. If new tools aren't better than what students already have, we don't need to use them.

- **Stay ahead of the competition:** While other companies introduce products around the same time as everyone else, Apple begins its design work two to three years before a product is released. By the time the Apple watch was unveiled, the company had been working on a wearable device for three years. Schools mustn't wait for others to come up with *next* practices for teaching and learning. Rather we need to dive into advance planning and design to stay on the cutting edge of our craft.

Who are the champions of innovation in your building? Do the right people join together to make new ideas irresistible? It's not *conversation* that makes ideas sticky— it's *engineering*. For a community of practice to thrive, exceptional people have to sustain it. Principals, counselors, staff developers, and teacher leaders who rely on a coalition of innovators set the stickiness factor in motion. Sticky innovation has a ripple effect.

Conclusion: Take a Walk on the Dog Side of Life

In 2013, O2, a telecommunications company in the United Kingdom, was looking to expand its digital products and service line. The first order of business was to raise enthusiasm about the advantages technology had to offer. To that end, O2 created a movement that infected the nation with an attitude of playfulness and positivity.

The company's first *Be More Dog* campaign featured a cat discovering his "dog side" as he transformed into an excitable puppy. While cats can be lazy and aloof, dogs love everything. Slippers? Amazing! People? Amazing! Chasing your tail? Amazing! A series of commercials and YouTube videos went viral as stoic British consumers were encouraged to shed their cat-like indifference and embrace O2 products with vigor and excitement. The original "Be More Dog" video (https://bit.ly/2O3i5vJ) racked up three million views and became the most shared advertisement in Great Britain's history.

Dogs live from moment to moment, processing information and acting upon it. If our mission is to expand the possibilities of learning, then we have to take more walks on the dog side of life. A cynic might argue that staying with what we know is safer. Yet, educators who become sensation seekers emulate an air of confidence and curiosity that's infectious. To unhinge innovation in schools, it's time to set our inhibitions aside. If other professions can do it, we can too.

The next chapter looks at learning and leadership experiences from a strengths-based perspective. Putting students, teachers, and administrators in situations where they feel successful makes them more likely to succeed. Chapter 3 charts a course to build upon the qualities, capacity, and connections of individuals and teams. Vignettes throughout the chapter aim to inspire readers in their pursuit of student empowerment and motivation.

Touchstone Takeaways

Consider the following Points to Ponder and Rapid-Fire Ideas on your own or within a teacher or leadership team to determine which innovative strategies might be implemented or scaled up in your workplace. The questions and activities in this section are designed to spark new ideas and help innovation flourish in your building or district.

Points to Ponder

1. How would you compare the environment in your classroom or school today with the vignette at the beginning of the chapter? What sounded familiar? What sounded different?

2. What elements of the design thinking framework do you find most compelling? Which elements are already present in your learning community?

3. Write down a dream you have for student learning. Write down a dream you have to grow as a professional. Consider the eight themes of practical dreaming presented in this chapter. Which theme(s) can you actualize to make your dreams a reality?

4. If you were to start a school from scratch, what would it look like? If the building had a voice, what would it say?

5. Reflect on some of the programs, products, and services in your school or district that have lacked staying power. Now think about things that have the stickiness factor. How were these sticky ideas engineered versus those that didn't last?

Rapid-Fire Ideas

Consider the following rapid-fire ideas as you begin implementing the ideas from this chapter in your classroom.

Play Mash Up

Educators are familiar with brainstorming. But the problem with brainstorming is that most teams think they do it well. IDEO posits that the key to better brainstorming is to get ridiculous (as opposed to practical) ideas flowing (Kelley, 2001). *Mash up* is a fast, fun way to spark fresh ideas by bringing odd or unexpected suggestions together. For example, to design a more student-centered education experience, your team might consider a mash up of a school and an amusement park. Mash ups start by identifying the challenge with a "How might we . . ." statement (for example, How might we improve the school experience for learners?). Then the team picks broad, unrelated categories (think pet stores and movie theaters) to mix up experiences. The goal is to think outside your industry and combine elements to come up with as many new services, products, or experiences as you can. To learn more about the mash up method, visit www.ideou.com/pages/ideation-method-mash-up (IDEO U, 2015).

Hold an Innovation Day

Set aside an entire day for students to create an innovation within a field of interest and publicly present a prototype by the end of the day. Innovations can range from building a Rube Goldberg machine to fashioning an everyday gadget that will make life easier. Two weeks before Innovation Day, ask students to complete a Planning Guide that describes their learning outcomes, materials, processes they'll follow, and the product they intend to create. After Innovation Day, provide students a Reflection Sheet to describe any challenges they encountered along with their overall experiences from the day. The internet is full of ideas surrounding the organization of a schoolwide or grade-specific Innovation Day.

Be More Dog

This activity is designed to open minds and present possibilities people may have been unable to see before. At your next team meeting, create different names for the list of items from a dog's point of view. For example, a UPS truck from a dog's perspective may be *Snacks on Wheels*. Take creative license to add to or modify the list. Have each team share their lists and give a prize to the funniest or most clever idea.

- Baby
- Siren
- The beach
- Shoe
- Vacuum cleaner
- Doggie daycare

Complete an Idea Grid

Think about what's going well in your school or district surrounding innovation, what could be better, what questions have surfaced, and what new ideas you'd like to try. Use the following template (figure 2.3) to record your reflections.

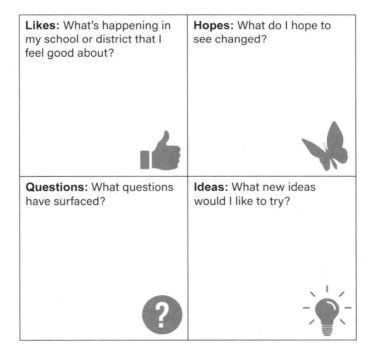

Figure 2.3: Idea grid—Bringing innovation to the surface.

*Visit **go.SolutionTree.com/21stcenturyskills** for a free reproducible version of this figure.*

Create an Affinity Map

How often do we give credence to what really matters to students (that is, our customers)? An affinity map (figure 2.4) offers a visual representation of what counts most. The map can come in any shape or size and be color coded for better organization. No matter what information you collect, you should always place the chief user's name in the center.

1. Create a four-quadrant layout on paper or a whiteboard. Meet with individuals or small groups of students (three to four maximum) to understand their inclination or opinions toward a particular topic, classroom activity, environmental set-up, or new idea.

2. Record students' comments, anecdotes, and quotes in the respective quadrant.

3. Align your implementation strategies, approaches, or environmental adaptations to learner desires or needs.

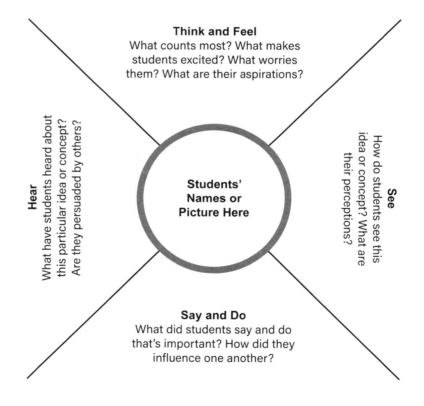

Figure 2.4: Affinity map—How do students see learning?

*Visit **go.SolutionTree.com/21stcenturyskills** for a free reproducible version of this figure.*

CHAPTER 3

Building a Strengths-Based Culture

When students not only know their strengths but more importantly apply them, the effect on their lives is transformational.
—CliftonStrengths for Students, Gallup

Let's assume Sophie, a junior, is trying to decide what she wants to do when she leaves high school. At this point, she either wants to be a teacher or a veterinarian. You consider Sophie to be a vociferous learner and observe her endless patience as she mentors others in class. You're also aware that Sophie loves animals and volunteers on weekends at the local animal shelter. Despite Sophie's inner drive, she's quite introverted. You worry that Sophie may lack the confidence and personality she'll need as a teacher. At the same time, you don't want to discourage her from pursuing her true passion.

Sophie's classmate Michael enjoys working with his hands. He can fix anything and has earned the nickname "MacGyver" from his peers. However, Michael's work habits leave much to be desired. With a C in physics, Michael's hopes of pursuing a STEM field might be in jeopardy. Despite excelling in lab work, Michael misses class assignments and needs prompting to turn in homework. Unfortunately, Michael's job at a local fast food restaurant leaves little time for co-curricular pursuits like participation on the robotics team or joining a study group.

And then there's Graciela. The child of immigrants, Graciela has been told since birth that she must go to college and get a good-paying job. Graciela's family has high hopes for her, a first-generation graduate, to become a doctor or lawyer. The dilemma is that Graciela has a passion for photography. As a founding member of the school's photo club and recent winner of a $2,000 scholarship for her entry in a community-sponsored photo contest, Graciela is rarely without her camera. She has confided in you that she's afraid to approach her parents about attending a photography school rather than a four-year university. Her recent scholarship money would easily cover first-semester expenses for a photography school if she lived at home.

The conundrum Sophie, Michael, and Graciela are facing isn't unique. Many students, along with their teachers and parents, believe if they don't earn straight As, the chances of a degree in the fields of science, law, mathematics, or other "respectable" professions are small. These careers tend to be reserved for the smartest of the smart. We know that each student is unique. But how often do we act on this uniqueness? As educators, our mission should be to help learners focus on the goals that will lead them to success while they're with us and after they leave us. Unless school systems shift attention away from GPAs and stop encouraging a "college for all" mindset, they will continue to disregard labor market realities, changing industry needs, and the employability potential of our graduates (Fleming, 2016). With rising postsecondary education costs and an oversaturation of graduates in some majors and underrepresentation in others, educators instead must guide students toward careers that are aligned with their strengths, interests, and values. Many districts have been so focused on four-year plans, college access, and high paying jobs that they've lost sight of the fact that students are struggling to make the connection between what they say they want in life and what they actually choose.

Rather than force all students down a path that may or may not suit them, this chapter encourages readers to prepare students for a modern workforce by tailoring teaching methods and assignments around learner strengths, interests, and passions. Schools should be a place where students are inspired by what they're learning and doing. Moreover, when students stretch themselves—even when something is hard or unfamiliar—it builds confidence and competence. *Strengths-based education*— the second touchstone of future-ready learning (see figure I.1, page 2)—is the process of assessing, teaching, and designing learning experiences that emphasize students' talents and enhance those talents through intellectual stimulation, academic development, and personal excellence (Rath, 2007). This chapter discusses five strategies for building a strengths-based culture.

1. Focusing on strong versus wrong
2. Developing leadership in teachers and students
3. Encouraging the zookeeper effect
4. Creating defining moments
5. Molding mindsets—theirs and ours

The chapter concludes with Points to Ponder and Rapid-Fire Ideas to kickstart educators on their journey to building a strengths-based culture. By implementing a curriculum that allows students to explore and apply their strengths, teachers can broaden content knowledge, build academic skills, and raise levels of engagement. When we take advantage of learner strengths as opposed to trying to fix their weaknesses, achievement soars.

⌐Ö¬ **PERSPECTIVES FROM THE FIELD**

It's long overdue to help our students, our families, and our neigh-bors in identifying a career path in line with who they are, what they're good at, and what the world will pay them to do.

—Kevin Fleming, author and community college instructor (2016, p. 27)

Focusing on Strong Versus Wrong

To clarify how a strengths-based instructional model might differ from what we see in a typical classroom, let's consider two scenarios. In the first scenario, fourth-grade teacher Elisa Jones conducts a fall reading assessment to determine students' deficits and gaps. She initiates interventions to improve academic shortcomings. Without focusing on problem areas, Ms. Jones is convinced her students won't attain reading mastery by the end of the year.

While most of Ms. Jones's students make adequate progress, five learners remain far below basic. Ms. Jones initiates a daily *double dip* in the Reading Lab and sends the students home with extra practice. With only eight weeks left in the school year, Ms. Jones is in a panic. She forms a *Fluency Five Club* and invites students to stay in at recess to practice sight words. Although everyone else in the class is reading chapter books, Ms. Jones borrows *The Boy Who Loved Words* (Schotter, 2006) from a first-grade teacher. She also decides to submit a Student Study Team (SST) referral to discuss special education testing for these five learners.

Across the hall is Sarah Barnett. Ms. Barnett recalls her own experiences in fourth grade when she was having trouble reading. Rather than remediate her deficits, Sarah's teacher reinforced reading elements she was good at and taught her how to apply these strengths to fill the gaps.

In her own class, Ms. Barnett invites struggling readers to use colored overlays and special lenses to improve their perception of words. One learner, who loves math-ematics, reads *Counting on Frank* by Rod Clement (1991). Another who is crazy about insects reads *Insect-Lo-Pedia* (Reinhart, 2003). Rewordify (rewordify.com)—a free online resource that improves fluency and comprehension—lets students click on replacement words, definitions, and a text-to-speech option as they read passages. Students use their smartphones and tablets to listen to Audible (www.audible.com) to read with their eyes and ears at the same time. A collection of high-interest books, historical documents, and classic literature is also available. The reading specialist spends thirty minutes each day in the classroom to provide additional support within the regular classroom environment. By building on students' strengths and daily successes, Ms. Barnett's struggling readers are actually learning more.

If students have to prevail over an area of weakness, using strengths to do it builds positive thinking. Conversely, students who are repeatedly pushed to fix a deficiency can feel broken and demoralized. An unwavering focus on what's strong versus what's wrong builds self-assured learners inside and outside of the school.

Students aren't the only ones who benefit from a strengths-based environment. According to the Gallup Organization, educators who intentionally discover their own talents and strengths at work are six times more likely to be engaged on the job than their counterparts who don't (Rath, 2007). While individual styles and approaches may differ, effective teachers and administrators make the most of their naturally recurring talents and apply these talents to boost their performance. Savvy administrators know that trying to fix people's weaknesses is like trying to teach a pig to sing—a waste of time and annoying to the pig.

 PERSPECTIVES FROM THE FIELD

We do not fit people into jobs. We find the best people and fit the jobs to them.

—Kelly Wilkins, deputy superintendent, *The Innovator's Mindset* (Couros, 2015, p. 129)

Strengths provide a foundation to do what we do best every day. They represent the activities that make us feel proud, strong, and happy. The acronym SIGN (success, instinct, growth, need) establishes shared meaning around strengths-based teaching, learning, and leadership (Buckingham, 2007).

- **Success:** The activity comes easy. We feel like we've always known how to do it. We may even take the activity for granted.

- **Instinct:** Instinct is drawn from an inner ability. When we're moving on instinct, it's hard to explain "how" we did something. Results seem automatic, almost without trying.

- **Growth:** Strengths continue to improve with repeated performance. It's easy to concentrate. Time passes quickly because we're so engrossed in what we're doing. This is where we find our flow.

- **Need:** The activity is very satisfying. We feel good when drawing upon our strengths and can't wait to do it again.

While strengths represent our ability to consistently complete a task with near-perfect performance, talents are patterns of thought, feeling, and behavior (Rath, 2007). These enduring elements occur naturally and can make our strengths stand out when applied in a productive way. Yet, talents cannot be learned or taught to the same degree of excellence as our strengths. We can find a compelling example in the story of Michael Jordan. Jordan is considered one of the most talented basketball players of all time. His individual accolades include six Most Valuable Player awards in six NBA championship wins, ten scoring titles, fourteen all-star appearances, and being a member of the U.S. Olympic Dream Team.

But in 1993, Michael Jordan lost his desire to play basketball and retired from the NBA. He then turned to baseball to fulfill a dream of his late father, who had always envisioned Michael as a major league player (NBA Staff, n.d.). However, when Jordan tried to leverage his talents in this new sport, he turned out to be an unspectacular performer. Just because someone is a strong athlete doesn't necessarily mean he or she can play any sport. The same holds true in education. An amazing first-grade teacher doesn't automatically make an amazing algebra teacher. Just because someone is the best assistant principal in the land doesn't guarantee he or she would be the best principal in the land.

To understand how it feels to perform a task you are good at in a different environment, take the following writing challenge in figure 3.1.

1. _____	1. _____
2. _____	2. _____
3. _____	3. _____
4. _____	4. _____
5. _____	5. _____

Figure 3.1: Writing challenge.

Pull out a piece of paper and number it as shown. Have a timer ready. On the right side of the paper sign your name five times in cursive just like you'd sign on a check or official document. Time yourself and record how long it took. Now switch to your nondominant hand and repeat the exercise on the left side of the paper. It's a race, so write as fast as you can.

When you used your dominant hand, what were you thinking? Did it feel natural and automatic? When you switched to your nondominant hand, what were you thinking? Did you know how to hold the pencil and form each cursive loop? Or was it awkward and uncomfortable? This exercise helps us discover what it's like to work on something when we apply our talents versus when we force our talents. Although we may be able to complete the task when we force our talents, it takes much longer and is of subpar quality.

Most students are told from a young age they can do anything if they set their minds to it. But this encouragement may actually do more harm than good (Liesveld & Miller, 2005). Clearly, if students practice hard, they can get better at a task. For example, members of the speech and debate team are usually better by their tenth competition than they were in their first. However, students can't be world-class in everything. Nor should we expect them to be. This insight, which is at the heart of strengths-based education, makes us more accepting of students' limitations. Although innate talents can't be instilled or removed, they can be identified and nurtured. Building relationships with students allows us to find out more about their hopes, dreams, and self-interests. In turn, we can explicitly connect lessons to pertinent skills and knowledge that activate intrinsic motivation.

Developing Leadership in Teachers and Students

There is near universal acknowledgment that the way schools are organized and managed—commonly referred to as school leadership—is crucial for student performance and academic outcomes (Ingersoll, Dougherty, & Sirinides, 2017). To that end, a long-standing goal of education reformers has been to involve several people in the work of leadership—starting with teachers and students—to decide and influence the outcomes together. While most educators would agree that an essential component of a strong school culture is effective leadership, few teacher education courses address leadership in their training programs. In fact, many teachers don't see themselves as leaders. Nor do they put much thought into sharing power with students to turn them into leaders themselves. Teachers generally believe it's their job to teach, the principal's job to lead, and the students' job to learn.

The development of student leaders is one of many promising approaches to building a strengths-based culture. Power is not a finite commodity. Nor is it reserved for those with a given title, age, charisma, or years of experience. When educators cultivate the leadership skills of students, they develop well-rounded youngsters who become leaders of themselves and others (Covey, Covey, Summers, & Hatch, 2014). The best principals, teachers, counselors, curriculum coaches, and staff developers don't just think *about* the future; they think *in* the future. A vision that's full of possibilities helps mold the environment necessary to achieve it. This is leadership.

Effective teacher leaders possess a variety of attributes that students, parents, and peers respect. They adapt their style to match each situation and group. Some attributes are part of one's personality, but they learn and refine others. Time and time again, we've seen teacher leadership elevate the very schools and systems in which they work. Leadership development is an area in which educators can become their own best teachers.

Purposeful interactions give teachers the power to lead change without leaving the classroom. Consider four lessons that will help light the way.

1. **Lesson 1: Be a multiplier**—Leaders come in two types: (1) multipliers and (2) diminishers (Wiseman, Allen, & Foster, 2013). Multipliers amplify the aspirations and capability of those around them. Diminishers, on the other hand, rely on their own expertise to control learning and relationships. In their haste to get things done, they ignore what others bring to the table. Educators with a multiplier mindset use their influence to create the conditions under which others flourish.

2. **Lesson 2: Take responsibility for the outcomes you get**—It can be tempting to take credit when things go well and to blame others when they don't. However, this pattern erodes trust and breeds unhealthy competition. Resourceful teacher leaders are neither credit grabbers nor blame throwers.

Instead, they respond positively to setbacks and treat mistakes as opportunities to learn and grow.

3. **Lesson 3: Listen and learn**—When teachers ask students about important topics like bullying, drug use, discrimination, and school connectedness, their opinions are insightful. Listening tours, advisory committees, and roundtable discussions draw students into the fold. Questions like, "What would make your experience here more meaningful?" invite critical thinking *about* school, not just *in* school.

4. **Lesson 4: Unleash the power of *yet***—In her research on growth mindsets, Carol S. Dweck (2006) shares how students "level up" when they say, "I'm not good at this . . . *yet*." As educators, we're expected to unleash the power of *yet* in learners. But it shouldn't stop there. We have to build *yet* language with colleagues too. Here's how it might sound: We don't have a solution to this challenge . . . *yet*. We aren't sure how to make this process easier . . . *yet*. We don't have all the resources . . . *yet*. Adding the word *yet* to a conversation says the answers are out there; we just need more time and effort to figure it out.

Because teachers tend to stay in the same school or district longer than administrators, their institutional knowledge is invaluable (School Leaders Network, 2014). However, it is only when teachers band together with their principal, peers, and students that the leadership culture is sown and grown. Leadership is action, not a position.

 PERSPECTIVES FROM THE FIELD

Together we have been able to transform the learning experience for thousands of children, leaving a legacy that has the potential to last for generations.

—Candace Singh (2016), superintendent, Fallbrook Union Elementary School District

When we turn to student leadership, we find that most schools offer leadership responsibilities to their learners (Covey et al., 2014). However, they generally bestow these responsibilities on the students who have proven themselves or were elected by their peers. What happens to the other 98 percent of the student body?

In the Fallbrook Union Elementary School District, teachers, principals, support staff, central office administrators, and the superintendent have joined forces to develop a culture of leadership that inspires every student and adult to be leaders in their own lives. Tucked away in the northernmost corner of San Diego County, the bucolic community is home to equestrian trails, avocado farms, nurseries, and the sprawling Marine Corps Base Camp Pendleton.

Using the *Leader in Me* model developed by Stephen and Sean Covey, educators teach the essential skills of accountability, adaptability, initiative, self-direction, responsibility, problem solving, communication, and teamwork in every classroom and every school beginning in kindergarten (Covey et al., 2014). Developed in partnership with teachers and administrators across the nation, the *Leader in Me* program equips learners with the leadership and life skills they need to succeed in the 21st century. Guided by the principles of interpersonal effectiveness and the premise that every child has the strengths and abilities to be a leader, the framework teaches students how to become self-reliant, plan ahead, set and track goals, express their viewpoints persuasively, resolve differences, value differences, and live a balanced life. The ultimate goal is to foster a schoolwide culture where student empowerment becomes a major driver of academic results.

The timeless *7 Habits* in table 3.1 are used to give students an immediate way to connect with their school and each other. This is especially important in a community like Fallbrook, since many children come from military and migrant farming families. Each habit reflects the personal attributes parents, teachers, the military community, and local businesses want to see developed in their students.

Fallbrook is the first school district in the United States to be recognized as a *Leader in Me* Lighthouse District, serving as a model of student leadership and empowerment. It has recorded dramatic changes: increased school connectedness, reduced absenteeism, fewer behavioral referrals, and increased academic achievement. According to Superintendent Candace Singh, the district has taken several intentional actions to sustain this strengths-based culture (C. Singh, personal communication, October 25, 2018).

- A strongly held belief among all adults in the potential of every student

- Ongoing staff training to reinforce common language grounded in the *7 Habits*

- Lighthouse Leadership Teams in every school to further develop and implement the *Leader in Me* approach throughout the district. Lighthouse teams are comprised of adults within a school—both teaching and non-teaching staff—who lead small action groups to accomplish academic and social-emotional goals and empower students to bring these goals to fruition in their everyday encounters.

- Partnership with FranklinCovey to provide a *Leader in Me* district coach that supports long-term implementation

- Ongoing training for parents in *The 7 Habits of Highly Effective Families* (Covey, 1998)

- Use of the *Thrively* strengths assessment (available at www.thrively.com /student) with every student to understand learner strengths, uncover potential career options, and align instructional approaches to these interests and options

- Student-led clubs based on student strengths, interests, and aspirations

- Career exploration activities to create a vision for the future

Table 3.1: 7 Habits of the *Leader in Me*

Habit	How It Looks and Sounds for Students
Habit 1: Be Proactive	• I have a "can do" attitude. • I choose my actions, attitudes, and moods. • I don't blame others. • I do the right thing without being asked, even if no one is looking.
Habit 2: Begin With the End in Mind	• I plan ahead and set goals. • I do things that have meaning and make a difference. • I am an important part of my classroom. • I look for ways to be a good citizen.
Habit 3: Put First Things First	• I spend my time on things that are important to me. • I say no to things I should not do. • I set priorities, make a schedule, and follow my plan. • I am organized.
Habit 4: Think Win-Win	• I want everyone to succeed. • I don't have to put others down to get what I want. • It makes me happy to see other people happy. • I like to do nice things for others. • When a conflict arises, I help brainstorm a solution. • We can all win!
Habit 5: Seek First to Listen, Then to Be Understood	• I listen to other people's ideas and feelings. • I try to see things from their viewpoints. • I listen to others without interrupting. • I am confident in voicing my ideas.
Habit 6: Synergize	• I value other people's strengths and learn from them. • I get along well with others, even people who are different from me. • I work well in groups. • I seek out other people's ideas to solve problems. • I know that two heads are better than one. • I am a better person when I let other people in my life and work.
Habit 7: Sharpen the Saw	• I take care of my body by eating right, exercising, and getting sleep. • I spend time with family and friends. • I learn in lots of ways and lots of places.

Source: Adapted from Covey et al., 2014, pp. 18–19.

The Fallbrook Union Elementary School District regularly hosts visitors from around the United States, who routinely comment on the leadership capacity of teachers and students. Employees throughout the district view leadership development as an ongoing process rather than a discrete set of lessons. Teachers recognize their responsibility to integrate a range of leadership roles in the classroom and beyond. With meaningful instructional practices galvanizing every building, educators teach and expect every Fallbrook learner to be an influencer in the workflow of his or her classroom and school life.

Instead of focusing on academic measures alone, readers are encouraged to explore the *Leader in Me* model or similar programs as a means to develop students' skills and confidence to successfully navigate a constantly changing world. When students have a seat at the table, campuswide improvements are made by students and for students. In turn, this creates an inclusive school climate where everyone matters and is empowered to make a difference.

Encouraging the Zookeeper Effect

Educators often use the fact that a student either keeps up with the class as a whole or falls behind to judge intelligence and ability (Robinson, 2015). One assumption is that students either have a good or a bad memory. Students with a bad memory have to work twice as hard to keep up. Yet, time and time again, students who struggle to memorize their multiplication tables have no problem memorizing the stats of, say, dozens of major league baseball players. "Bad" memories are more likely due to lack of interest in school than lack of capacity.

To understand the dichotomy between the joy and the agony of learning, let's consider the example of zookeepers. Zookeepers have a tough job. Animals get hurt, grow old, and eventually die. There's no easy zoo animal, despite some being more docile than others. Zookeepers wash dishes, sweep floors, and clean up lots of excrement. Despite such seemingly unpleasant working conditions, scholars describe the profession as one of the most satisfying jobs on the planet (Bunderson & Thompson, 2009). Zookeepers move across the country and make huge sacrifices to earn 50 percent less than the national average for occupations that require similar training and education. How can this be?

Zookeepers find meaning in unglamorous tasks like cleaning enclosures because they're filled with a sense of purpose. They consider these tasks to have *intrinsic value*. Not only do animals rely on them to survive, in some cases zookeepers are saving an entire species. The job has been described as a divine calling (Bunderson & Thompson, 2009). Zookeepers also report that their work produces a constant state of flow—freedom, variety, clear tasks, and feedback—because they're doing it for the animals.

Grown-ups are forever extolling a litany of reasons why a good education is important in a young person's life. Forcing students to plug away at repetitive activities or mindless homework is often deemed necessary for students to receive an education that will help them achieve their life goals. Clearly, education plays a central role in improving the future prospects of students, thereby strengthening our economy and society. But how can we avoid the bane of K–12 schooling—boredom—and ensure all students experience joyful learning? Is it possible to perpetuate the zookeeper effect in every building?

Reorienting a school's culture to promote a sense of purpose takes planning. To expedite the process, we write SMART (strategic and specific, measurable, attainable, results-oriented or relevant, and time bound) goals for nearly every subject and lesson. Although these goals set out to improve overall academic performance, they are rarely co-developed with students or used at the classroom level to elevate learning (O'Neill & Conzemius, 2006). While SMART goals may motivate some students, they don't activate purposeful learning in most students. For example, if a student is a great artist, it's rare to find teachers nurturing these talents. Instead, we may hear, "If you finish your writing assignment early, you can draw for a few minutes." Along the same lines, if a student struggles in math, a common practice is to assign extra math problems for homework. Couros (2015) explains, "We dangle student's interests in front of them like a carrot. We say, 'You can only do what you love when you finish that which you hate'" (p. 124). Such prescriptive targets and rigidity can actually dull students' natural interests and curiosity. While SMART goals provide a yardstick for learning, they can inadvertently cause educators to fixate on a narrow skillset that keeps students from reaching their full potential.

Hardie (2019) points out that adult perceptions of education "are clouded by the way we *hope* students experience our schools, missing, at times the hard truths of students' day-to-day experiences, both inside and outside of school" (p. 18). Consider six strategies to leverage learner talents and infuse activities with intrinsic value.

1. **Connect the dots:** Tell students how their efforts fit the broader context. Be clear on three things: (1) the point of having a learning goal; (2) the ways you'll support each student in achieving it; and (3) what's in it for students if they do.

2. **Design the right tasks:** If we want students to do things with quality above the norm, we have to provide them with the right tasks. As the architect of these tasks, set parameters so that students aren't overwhelmed by all there is to learn. At the same time, give students creative license to get to the place you want them to end up.

3. **Cultivate curiosity:** While many teachers labor to write engaging lesson plans, these efforts don't always reap the benefits one hopes for. A better approach is to find out what students are curious about. What are their passions? For example, ask students to identify a problem in their own school or community, then structure your instruction around this dilemma. Standards will always play a role. But teachers shouldn't feel confined by narrow paths to meet them.

4. **Establish an atmosphere of relaxed intensity:** Relaxed intensity comes from pushing students to achieve academic goals with a smile, laughter, and

a twinkle in their eye. A combination of healthy competition (for example, We're going to be the best class in the school!) with shared levity will net a greater sense of purpose.

5. **Bolster imagination:** Imagination is the cornerstone of creativity. Allow students to enter make-believe worlds to prompt deeper understanding of complex topics. Pretend and play isn't just for preschoolers. Invite students to produce videos, write stories, and design products to feed their curious minds.

6. **Share sparkling moments:** Students remember our narrative when we share sparkling moments that have nothing to do with test scores. Collect stories from students and parents that convey hope and inspiration. Sparkling moments provide a wonderful counterbalance to daily classroom realities.

Future-ready learners thrive in environments where they want to learn and where teachers encourage them to discover their true passions. For some educators, this represents a different way of working with students. Practical activities to align students' strengths, interests, and values toward important goals are a surefire way to set the zookeeper effect in motion.

Creating Defining Moments

In *The Power of Moments*, Chip and Dan Heath (2017) argue that our lives are measured in moments. Defining moments not only provoke temporary happiness, like laughing at a friend's joke, but also create "peaks" that transcend the normal course of events. For instance, the dopamine rush that follows a ride on Disney's Space Mountain may be one of those moments. The first standing ovation as the lead in the school play might be another. In a matter of seconds, the sensory pleasure we feel turns an ordinary moment into something extraordinary.

The science of defining moments has revealed that we don't need to leave these events to chance (Heath & Heath, 2017). In fact, teachers can boost their impact on learning by fostering more defining moments in the classroom. The four elements in figure 3.2 underscore a defining moment. While some moments may contain all four elements, only one element has to be present to conjure a lasting memory.

Let's explore the four elements in more detail. First, defining moments rise above everyday activities to produce an extreme sense of joy, engagement, or motivation. This *elevation* comes from transitions, social occasions, performances, presentations, and milestones.

A transformative discovery or "aha" triggers the second element, *insight*. Perhaps it's a quote or article that moves you. Or you hear a podcast that changes your world-view. Journal writing and mentorships are other sources where insights can lead to defining moments.

Pride, the third element of a defining moment, captures us at our very best. We experience pride through courage, perseverance, or achievement. Finishing your first

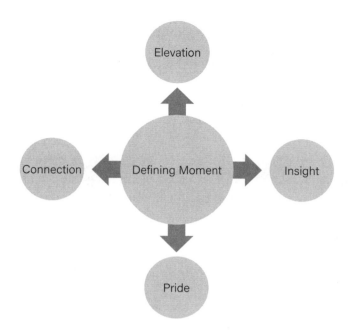

Source: Adapted from Heath & Heath, 2017.

Figure 3.2: Four elements of defining moments.

10k race, getting a promotion, standing up to a bully, or being honored as educator of the year are just a few examples.

Last but not least, our *connection* with others solidifies our defining moments. Weddings, graduations, bat or bar mitzvahs, vacations, sporting events, or work triumphs bind people together. Whether we knew these people previously or a unique circumstance brought us together, we form bonds through shared meaning and feeling like part of a greater mission.

Even as standardized testing looms in schools like a hungry tiger, it's possible for educators to become the authors of defining moments. What if you introduced a ceremony that students would remember for a lifetime? What if you turned a student's moment of despair into a moment of triumph? What if you assigned a project that promoted the inherent respect of others and helped students realize they can't accomplish everything on their own? Educators around the country are shaping learners' daily lives with defining moments. Two examples of these are Senior Signing Day and Genius Projects, which I discuss in the following sections.

Senior Signing Day

An example of this comes from Houston, Texas. In 1997, Houston teacher Chris Barbic founded YES Prep, a public charter school serving low-income Latino families. In 2000, Barbic and his colleague Donald Kamentz came up with the idea of Senior Signing Day after watching top high school athletes sign their college football acceptance letters on ESPN (Heath & Heath, 2017). As the two educators tuned in to the television coverage, Kamentz noted, "It blows my mind that we celebrate athletes this way, but we don't have anything that celebrates academics in the same way" (Heath & Heath, 2017, pp. 1–2). At that moment, Barbic and Kamentz decided that the underserved students in their school—many of whom would be the first in their families to finish high school and go on to college—deserved cheers and celebrations too.

In April 2001, Barbic held the first Senior Signing Day in the school gymnasium. Three hundred students and staff cheered on seventeen graduating seniors and their families. As each senior took the stage, they proudly announced where they would be attending college in the fall. For added suspense, some graduates decided to keep their final college decision a secret from friends. As they pulled out a T-shirt or pennant to heighten the reveal, the crowd erupted in applause. After the onstage ceremony, students were joined by family members for the official signing of matriculation letters, confirming their fall enrollment in college. By 2019, YES Prep enrollment had grown to 13,000 students in grades 6–12 occupying eighteen campuses in the greater Houston area (YES Prep Public Schools, n.d.). Senior Signing Day has become so successful that it now takes place in the Toyota Center, home of the Houston Rockets basketball team.

But Senior Signing Day is only the beginning of the success strategies at YES Prep. It's one thing to have students enroll in college, but another for them to finish. The fact that over 90 percent of YES Prep students are first-generation college students creates a unique set of challenges for youngsters as they enter and matriculate through the system. One challenge may be getting parents to agree to allow their sons and daughters to attend college out of state—a practice not readily accepted among some families or cultures. Another challenge is the availability of financial aid.

To remove obstacles, YES Prep has entered into formal partnerships with a diverse group of colleges and universities. Through these partnerships, the colleges have agreed to enroll students in *cohorts* to reduce their sense of isolation. Cohorts serve as mutually supportive communities within the larger campus environment and give added peace of mind to parents. Not only do partner institutions provide emotional and academic support to YES graduates, they offer full-ride scholarships to ease any financial hardships on families.

Life-changing moments like Senior Signing Day not only enhance students' school experience, they are also rich in emotion. These flagship memories bring to bear how important it is to help students set purposeful goals that align with their passions and dreams. As students experience defining moments in school, it strengthens their understanding of themselves and their world. These experiences might parlay into getting into the right college to pursue a love of music, having the confidence to move to another state after graduation to develop independence, or collaborating with peers who share similar interests. Educators play a huge role in making sure students stumble upon things they're inspired to pursue. The value of serendipity cannot be overstated in the journey to build a strengths-based learning culture.

 PERSPECTIVES FROM THE FIELD

> Senior Signing Day is a chance to celebrate my success and is a stepping stone to college. I'll be the first to graduate, so I'll be a role model for my younger siblings and cousins. I'm grateful to my parents because they convinced me to stay in AP classes when I thought I couldn't do it. I also want to thank my college counselor for helping me through the financial process and everyone who helped us through Hurricane Harvey. People provided supplies to relieve the burden at home and allowed me to focus on school.
>
> —Reyna, 2018 graduate, North Central YES Prep (YES Prep, 2018)

Genius Projects

Sage Creek High School in Carlsbad, California, stands as another compelling example where defining moments happen. Along with AP classes, homework, and extracurricular commitments, students take on an additional obligation to graduate: all seniors must complete a Genius Project based on a subject they're passionate about. Modeled after the business practice used at Google, *Genius Projects* give students the chance to explore their interests, hone their skills, and bring an idea to fruition. Student projects have ranged from teaching senior citizens the art of dance, to designing iPad carts that can sterilize and recharge devices, to developing real-life models of stem cell therapy, to assembling comfort kits for foster youth (Brennan, 2018).

Since opening the school in 2013, the faculty and administration have maintained a shared belief that all students have a passion that drives them. At the same time, the school's vision is to create an interconnected learning community that prepares students to thrive as responsible citizens in an ever-changing world. Providing students the time, platform, and structure to wonder and give back is part of the Sage Creek experience.

Beginning in junior year, every student picks an area to learn more about. English teachers serve as project managers. Students must also find a content mentor to assist them in fleshing out and shaping ideas. Content mentors are professionals in the field not affiliated with the school.

Before getting the green light to begin their Genius Project, students must pitch their idea to a panel of peers, parents, and teachers. The pitch must describe timelines, steps, resources, and a justification for their choices. The imperative is that students deepen their understanding of themselves through research and methodologies that bring about opportunities for change. Rather than trying to find a cure for cancer or ending human trafficking, students receive encouragement to showcase how amazing and unique they are. The skills they gain throughout the project teach students that they can transform the smallest hobby or interest into a vessel for good. At Sage Creek, boosting students' confidence and passion is the gateway to intrinsic motivation.

PERSPECTIVES FROM THE FIELD

We say to our students, "Look around you. What is needed? What do you notice that you want to change?" . . . We hope that this project extracts meaningful purpose from what our students are already doing and from the passions they already have.

—Shannon Alberts, teacher, Sage Creek High School (Lovely, 2016)

Throughout the two-year journey, English teachers grade students based upon various benchmarks and deliverables. Benchmarks act as checkpoints whereby teachers ensure students have a solid grasp on content and skills before moving on. Benchmarks might involve technical reading, research, data collection, or basic design elements. Each benchmark is tied to a deliverable. Deliverables are pieces of work students turn in for formative assessment and feedback. Examples of deliverables include storyboards, scripts, research documents, outlines, diagrams, sketches, drafts, letters of solicitation, interview data, and so on.

Embedding the Genius Project into an existing course like English eliminates the dilemma teachers face with trying to coordinate joint assignments. It's also a course every student takes every year. During junior and senior year, students devote their class time to making calls, working out logistical details, filling out permits and paperwork, and incorporating digital tools into their projects.

As seniors, students present their discoveries through videos and a school showcase. For the culminating event, classmates vote on the top sixty Genius Projects. A panel of outside judges then reviews the top projects and narrows the field to eight finalists. The school invites the eight finalists to present their Genius Project journey at a TED-style symposium in front of hundreds of parents, students, community members, and local reporters. Reilly Cornwall, a 2018 finalist who spent a year photographing homeless youth in San Diego County, summed up her insights with a level of maturity that transcended her youthful demeanor: "Never make assumptions about people because you never know what's going on in their life. Everyone has a story. Always be kind and respectful no matter what the circumstances are" (Sage Creek High School, n.d.).

Senior Signing Day and the Genius Projects are just two examples of how to generate defining moments in the classroom. Through elevation, insight, connections, and pride, students experience life-altering encounters that are hard to forget.

Molding Mindsets—Theirs and Ours

Scientists have known for some time that the brain is like a muscle: the more it's used, the stronger it gets (Central Michigan University, n.d.). Prominent scholar Carol S. Dweck (2010) applies this knowledge to show how the mindsets of students and educators can be molded to improve learning. While a fixed mindset says, "Once I'm done, I'm done," a growth mindset says, "I love a challenge" (Dweck, 2010, p. 16).

Students with a growth mindset possess the courage and determination to tackle weaknesses. They view challenging work as a chance to learn and grow. Conversely, students with a fixed mindset are comfortable with the current limits on what they know. They will often bypass important opportunities to learn if these opportunities may lead to poor performance or force them to admit their deficiencies (Dweck, 2010). A teacher's own mindset messages affect students' feelings of competence, connectedness, and perceived support (see table 3.2). When teachers convey inclusive messages of growth and potential into their daily practice, they're able to counter fixed mindset behaviors.

Table 3.2: How Teacher Mindset Looks and Sounds in the Classroom

Teacher Mindset Messages	Growth Orientation	Fixed Orientation
Success	• Praises students' efforts and strategies • Teaches students to relish a challenge • Highlights strengths so students can take advantage of what they already do well • Treats students equitably	• Praises students for being "smart" • Teaches students to find the right answer • Highlights deficits so students will know which gaps to fill • Treats students equally
Belonging	• Positions students for collaborative learning • Refers to it as "our" classroom • Avoids comparisons to other students	• Positions students for independent learning • Refers to it as "my" classroom • Makes comparisons to other students
Purpose	• Connects lessons to bigger picture and real life • Provides practice that resonates with learners • Encourages experimentation over accuracy	• Connects lessons to pacing guides and standards • Provides practice from the textbook • Encourages accuracy over experimentation

continued ➲

Teacher Mindset Messages	Growth Orientation	Fixed Orientation
Affirmation	• Uses checkpoints to assess growth • Emphasizes persistence and learning-to-learn skills for all students • "Teaches up" no matter student's language, culture, race, socioeconomic status, or other characteristics	• Uses grades and scores to assess performance • Emphasizes persistence and learning-to-learn skills mainly to weaker students • "Teaches down" based on student's language, culture, race, socioeconomic status, or other characteristics

Source: Adapted from Association for Supervision and Curriculum Development (ASCD), 2011, and Hennessey, 2018.

Dweck's (2006) studies have homed in on three elements of classroom culture that give students a reason to try. First is the "good struggle." In a classroom where the good struggle holds sway, students grapple with issues and come up with their own solutions. When they find themselves at a dead end, they look for other strategies. As they attain their goals, students develop persistence and resilience. Teachers offer effort-based praise and use struggles to deepen understanding of concepts. For instance, the teacher might say, "There's nothing wrong with being wrong. It's pivotal to your learning. Where would you like to go next?" Finally, students work on tasks they believe are worth completing. Instead of assigning easier work to struggling students, teachers provide various entry points to position all students for success.

A second element to keep students from giving up is the gift of time. We know that fast learning is not necessarily the best learning. In fact, when students take longer to complete a task, they understand it at a higher level (Dweck, 2006). Rather than telling students, "Hurry up and finish your work," growth-oriented teachers encourage learners to proceed thoughtfully. They resist the pressure to cover new material. They teach students to slow down by realistically pacing their assignments. They scaffold thinking by asking questions without stepping in to do the work. They introduce students to historical figures who weren't "fast" learners. Albert Einstein, for example, pondered the same questions year after year (Dweck, 2010). And it's a good thing he did!

The third element is responsible risk taking. If we want students to take more risks, we must convince them that we welcome and expect mistakes in the classroom. We should emphasize effort over perfection. Because students generally equate failure with intellectual inferiority, students tend to fixate on success. Changing our reaction to mistakes and failure reduces the pressure students feel to be right.

According to a 2016 national study conducted by *EdWeek*, 98 percent of all teachers believe that integrating a growth mindset into their practices will lead to improved student learning (Education Week Research Center, 2016). Yet, only 20 percent of the respondents felt they were good at doing it. Experts worry that teachers have developed misconceptions about a growth mindset that, when put into practice, could actually undermine the theory's effectiveness (Education Week Research Center, 2016). For example, one reported misconception is that teachers continue to place emphasis on praising student efforts instead of praising their learning strategies. Another concern is that teachers who have labeled students "difficult to teach" may perceive these students to have a fixed mindset (p. 4). When teachers pin a student's struggles or apathy on a fixed mindset, they inadvertently neglect to provide tasks that will challenge these learners in a meaningful way.

When students get stuck, they need to draw upon a repertoire of approaches. Sheer effort alone won't stimulate improvement. Simple changes in the classroom can foster an environment in which students are not only aware of growth mindset strategies, but actively partake in cultivating them. Here are four tips to get the ball rolling (Ferlazzo, 2012).

1. **Tell students why you're challenging them:** When introducing a new topic say, "This concept will cause you to stretch your thinking. The reason I'm challenging you is to wake up your creativity. If idea X is uninspiring, there are twenty-five more letters in the alphabet."

2. **Turn defeatist self-talk into positive dialogue:** Create a *What Can I Say to Myself?* poster with two headings: "Instead of Saying This . . ." and "I Will Think This." On the left side, have students make a list of the defeatist statements they commonly make (for example, I'm not good at this. This is too hard. I'll never be as smart as so-and-so). On the right side, invite students to identify what they might think or say instead (for example, What am I missing? This task is going to take a little more time and effort. I'll see what a classmate does and use these strategies myself).

3. **Use reverse brainstorming:** Many of us believe that reducing pollution is beneficial to the environment or that studying hard will lead to better grades. But how about asking students to brainstorm ideas about why we should *increase* pollution or study *less*? Generating ideas contrary to popular belief builds fluency and flexibility. For example, if bullying is a schoolwide issue, ask students to identify all the ways to increase bullying. Ideas might include things like posting mean comments online, promoting a name-calling day, and so on. This approach is especially effective when students have become cynical or indifferent toward solving a crucial problem. Generating negative solutions actually helps students develop a more open mind and pursue ideas that traditional thinking tends to overlook. In essence, reverse brainstorming promotes original ideas that may feel wrong, but ultimately can lead to something right.

4. **Focus feedback and praise on process rather than product:** In our results-driven climate, this may seem counterintuitive. However, many

things beyond high scores are important to learning. Challenge seeking and problem finding breed success too. Giving feedback and displaying work products around these competencies push students to see the value of their actions. Moreover, when we assess and praise students for things like grit and resilience, we emphasize that these attributes are within their control.

Real learning starts when students feel stuck. Mistakes serve as diagnostic tools to tell students what they still need to learn. While the differences may seem subtle, they can forever change how students interpret and respond to situations. Since students' brains are malleable, it's up to us to shift our classroom culture to mold, bend, and reshape them. As students struggle productively, and then overcome their struggles, their strengths stand out and their weaknesses become less relevant.

Conclusion: Wise Up

"Chloe has so much potential, but can't seem to live up to it"; "It's a shame Malcolm isn't able to put his talents to better use"; "We have a talent crisis in our country." These are just a few examples of the proclamations we might hear around the notion of untapped potential. As humans, we admire talent and wish we had more of it ourselves. Child prodigies amaze us because we compare them to other children the same age. We see their cute faces and forget their brains have been shaped by extensive practice. If people had compared young Mozart to older musicians with thousands of hours of practice instead of to other six-year-olds, he may not have seemed all that exceptional (Syed, 2010).

Where does this leave educators in relation to the ability to ignite the genius in every student? Talent in and of itself is an overrated concept. Top performers aren't born with sharper instincts in the same way that chess masters don't have superior memories (Syed, 2010). Students who are labeled "talented" and "smart" begin to identify with these labels, leaving them more vulnerable in the face of adversity or criticism (Dweck, 2006).

It's time to wise up to the fact that talent is everywhere in schools. Students develop it when mental acuity, emotional intelligence, and purposeful practice are mixed in the same pot. The capacity to believe in every learner's ability is a powerful performance enhancer. Requiring students to clock oodles of hours on mundane activities (such as writing out spelling words five times each) won't jolt motivation.

Experts claim that in order to master complex tasks, one has to invest approximately ten thousand hours of quality practice (Gladwell, 2008; Syed, 2010). While this figure may sound extreme, when broken down it amounts to ninety minutes of practice per day for twenty years. The good news is that students are with us for thirteen years. With roughly 16,380 hours of K–12 schooling, there's no reason we can't challenge students beyond current limits to feed their appetite for learning. It's not a matter of having enough time in school, it's a matter of using the time we have wisely. When students engage in consequential tasks for longer and harder periods, there is no question they'll get better.

In the next chapter, I will traverse different pathways to deliver tailor-made, personalized learning opportunities. I will present varied contexts and models to enlist student participation and consent in their own learning. I will also discuss core components and philosophies of personalization to create systemic shifts that go farther, wider, and deeper than schools and districts have gone before.

Touchstone Takeaways

Consider the following Points to Ponder and Rapid-Fire Ideas on your own or within a teacher or leadership team to discern which strengths-based approaches can be implemented in your school or district. The questions and activities in this section are designed to spark new conversations to enable students, teachers, and school leaders to soar with their strengths.

Points to Ponder

1. What are the current strengths of your school? What activities happen in your building to ensure learners are fully engaged thinkers who remain the motivated, joyful people they were before they started school?

2. Think of an occasion when you responded to a student in a way that may have rationalized his or her perceived weaknesses. Contemplate how this response might have limited this student's progress. What would you say or do differently next time?

3. Select a lesson you plan to teach in the upcoming week. Write down all the elements of the lesson that give it intrinsic value (that is, the zookeeper effect). How will this lesson bring out the genius in every learner? How might you adjust the lesson for struggling learners? Once the lesson is finished, have students describe the "magic elements" that made them excited to learn. Magic elements include things in the lesson that awakened students' minds, produced joy or delight, or were deemed purposeful in nature.

4. Think of a defining moment when you were in school. What made this moment stand out? What defining moments have you experienced in your career? Which elements (elevation, insight, pride, connection) were present to conjure up such lasting memories?

5. If your principal or a colleague were to visit your classroom tomorrow, what would he or she see or hear to evaluate the degree to which you promote a "good struggle" environment? Make a list of the different ways you're able to help students understand that errors and mistakes open doors to learning.

Rapid-Fire Ideas

Consider the following rapid-fire ideas as you begin implementing the ideas from this chapter in your classroom.

Conduct a Leadership Flashlight

Make a list of leadership attributes that are part of your personality. Create a second list of the attributes you'd like to develop or refine. In this second list, include components from the four lessons that make leaders shine: (1) be a multiplier; (2) share responsibility; (3) listen and learn; and (4) use the power of *yet* (page 45). Based on both lists, write down three leadership goals that will help you effect meaningful change in your classroom or school.

Engage in a Mindset Makeover

It's important to reflect on fixed mindset practices from the past and learn how to change the internal monologue that frames these practices. Taking risks with lessons, asking colleagues for feedback, and growing as professionals may call for a makeover. Watch Michael Jordan's *Failure* commercial (https://bit.ly/1fy4QMh). Create a mantra or motto that personifies your positive inner voice. Share this mantra with students and colleagues. Invite them to notify you if you break your own rules.

Pursue Project Wonder

Project Wonder connects students from all over the world to share things they care about and want to get involved in. Log into the Wonderment website at https://thewonderment.com/projects to have your class join an existing path. You can use these paths to connect your students with other groups to grow a project that's already underway. Or your class can pursue its own Project Wonder fueled by a "wondermeter," which includes outside resources to help the project grow. The goal of the Wonderment is to provide shared space where students' interests and ideas can transform the world.

Consider Famous Failures

Many people are unaware that Walt Disney was fired from a newspaper because he lacked imagination. The Beatles experienced similar rejection when Decca Records refused to sign them because "guitar groups were on their way out" (CBS News, n.d.). Share one or two famous failures with students. Assign students to groups to research other well-known figures that faced setbacks or rejection and present their findings. This activity helps learners recognize that many famous people have had to overcome obstacles and persevere in order to achieve success.

Take the RIASEC Interest Survey

Psychologist John Holland found that most people fit one of six personality types: (1) Realistic, (2) Investigative, (3) Artistic, (4) Social, (5) Enterprising, and (6) Conventional—collectively referred to by the acronym RIASEC (figure 3.3; Jones, 2014). The RIASEC assessment, available online at https://openpsychometrics.org/tests/RIASEC, has been used in both education and work settings to link an individual's preferences for situations and activities to his or her environment. According to studies, the closer students choose a college major or career that aligns with their

Holland personality type, the more likely they are to succeed (Jones, 2014). In addition to the RIASEC assessment, a variety of instruments is available on the internet to help students assess and discover their interests, including the SkillScan (2011; available at https://bit.ly/2kt9E0d). Take this assessment yourself or administer it to your students to help them identify their strengths and potential careers of interest.

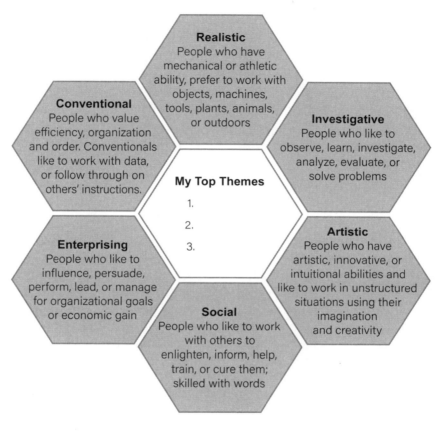

Source: Adapted from World of Work, n.d.

Figure 3.3: RIASEC themes.

CHAPTER 4

Designing Personalized Experiences

[Personalized learning] is not about baiting a hook. It's about helping
students find their spark and make their own fire.
—Larry Ferlazzo, Award-Winning Teacher, Burbank, California

With the growing demand for customization in consumer products, the simple fact is that off-the-shelf items are no longer our sole option. Mass adoption of services like Netflix, Amazon, and Pandora has created a new mindset for consumers: "Let me watch it, buy it, and listen to it my way." A fundamental marketing strategy for companies seeking growth is letting customers know they're paying attention.

When we compare trends in retail marketing to trends in education, we see similar demands. Growing consumer expectations have prompted retailers to find other ways to personalize shopping experiences. Reward programs, mobile apps that help shoppers access coupons and streamline pharmacy orders, curbside pick-up, and free shipping are just a few ways retailers are meeting customer demands. Convenience, low cost, and customization are the backbone of success in a changing consumer market. In schools, educators are involved in parallel pursuits. Teachers and administrators are asking crucial questions and exploring options to capture the power of personalization in the classroom.

We've all heard the term *personalized learning* at one time or another, but we may have seen it defined differently. For the purposes of this book, I use the definition proposed by Jim Rickabaugh (2016) in *Tapping the Power of Personalized Learning*, which states:

> [Personalized learning is] an approach to learning and instruction that is designed around individual learner readiness, strengths, needs, and interests. Learners are active participants in setting goals, planning learning paths,

> tracking progress, and determining how learning will be demonstrated. At any given time, learning objectives, content, methods, and pacing are likely to vary from learner to learner as they pursue proficiency aligned to established standards. A fully personalized environment moves beyond differentiation and individualization. (p. 6)

While the concept of personalized learning has gained momentum in education, author and thought leader Carol Ann Tomlinson (2017) warns, "It's unwise to assume any model [of personalization] will work for learners of all ages, in all subjects" (p. 12). So many iterations of personalized learning now exist that the concept has begun to look like everything and nothing (Tomlinson, 2017).

With no shortage of schools and districts trying to reach the personalized learning mountaintop, it's prudent to reflect on the catalysts that actually make the model work. The beliefs, forethought, and planning necessary to introduce and institutionalize this type of change are extensive. New ecosystems cannot grow or scale without those who implement them first looking deeper.

Today's technology-driven life exposes humans to rapid change. Adolescents are eager to embrace these changes. As such, the possibilities for personalization in the classroom are limited only by our imagination. Yet, in reality, the best approaches become less personal when teachers carry them out without student participation or consent. While there is no simple on and off switch to power up personalization, specific shifts are required to increase student engagement, ownership, and persistence. A fundamental purpose of personalized learning is to let students know we've taken notice of their needs and aspirations and we're fully committed to building their capacity to learn.

This chapter focuses on the third touchstone: designing personalized experiences (see figure I.1, page 2). It begins by introducing seven questions to kickstart the personalization process. The chapter then outlines several strategies readers can choose from to initiate more personalized experiences in their classroom or school. It concludes with Points to Ponder and Rapid-Fire Ideas to consider individually or in learning teams to leverage instructional strategies that will lead to a more personalized learning environment.

Seven Questions to Kickstart the Process

The cumulative impact of motivation, efficacy, engagement, and ownership can equip students with crucial tools to become self-directed, independent learners (Rickabaugh, 2016). Students value the power to choose, whether it be the sports they play, the hobbies they take up, the clothes they wear, the music they listen to, or the subjects they study in school. However, before schools can tailor learning experiences to student yearnings, teachers and administrators must recognize and reflect on the complexity of such structures.

While most versions of customization are instructional in nature, the benefits for students vary from school to school and classroom to classroom. Tomlinson (2017) has developed a list of questions educators can ask to take informed action. The goal isn't to fully answer each question, but rather to raise awareness of the intricacies a shift of this nature might generate. These seven questions will help educators contemplate a sustainable implementation process.

1. **Why personalized learning, and why now?** Without a clear reason to introduce this approach, people will become mired in the *what* and the *how*. Staff motivation and investment in personalization can only derive from the *why*.

2. **What will the match be between curriculum and personalization?** It's unwise to select curriculum without knowing which type of experiences you're committed to offer. This is akin to trying to cross the ocean on a bicycle (Tomlinson, 2017). You must know the vision before starting your journey. Once the learning vision is clear, you can decide which learning platforms (digital, project based, independent study, blended, and so on) are best suited to deliver the curriculum.

3. **Who will experience personalization, and when will they experience it?** One can never assume that any approach will work for every learner in every grade in every subject. Determining who the audience is and whether personalization will occur all day or for a portion of the day allows for balanced integration and implementation. Starting small with department- or grade-level volunteers is more apt to gain traction than forced implementation on a whole-district or whole-school basis.

4. **What supports will teachers need?** Many teachers will find the process liberating after years of being handcuffed by prescribed curricula, pacing guides, and standards-based materials. Other teachers will find it unsettling. It's impossible to know out of the gate what safety nets and hand holding teachers may need.

5. **Who'll help teachers reimagine and retool?** Schedules, grading, assessments, support services, and room environments are just a few things that teachers will need to rethink in a personalized learning environment. Without staff expertise, team leaders, and just-in-time professional development, a paradigm shift will be hard to sustain.

6. **What's the principal's role, and where will he or she find support?** Just as the role of teachers has been shaped by standardization and uniformity, the role of building principals has evolved in the same manner. School leaders must alter their beliefs and practices from a teacher-centric orientation to a student-centric orientation. How will the leader handle skepticism, resistance, and setbacks? And who will be there to boost up the principal along the way?

7. **Where are parents in the process?** While some parents will openly embrace the concept, others may find personalized learning *fuzzy*. Teachers must support parents to help them gain a realistic understanding of what personalization is and isn't. They'll want to know how repositioning their child within the instructional process is going to make him or her more successful. When all is said and done, parents care most if their children are safe and happy and can keep up with their peers.

These questions remind us that applying personalized learning can leave a trail of unintended consequences. For instance, teaching from the sidelines might make teachers feel they are neglecting their duties. Giving up classroom control without building learner commitment may lead to more discipline problems. Keeping track of individual students and their assignments can overwhelm teachers, especially if they don't enlist students to share this responsibility. Nonetheless, our familiarity with the past should not cause us to ignore the demands of the present. Customization in the classroom is the gateway to students' futures. Not only does it build confidence and commitment toward skillful interdependence, it takes advantage of students' natural disposition to learn.

As a grand design, personalized learning calls for a clear vision and distinguishable process to re-prioritize the way educators think and work. Teachers' personal stances on whether they "have to" or "want to" engage in these processes will determine student outcomes no matter which path is taken. Thus, it is important to help teachers acquire the tools and training they need before you launch personalized initiatives in your building or district.

Core Components of Personalization

On most days in schools across America, teachers prepare lessons based on factors other than what each student may need, want, or be ready for. Pacing guides, state testing windows, locally created benchmarks, grade-level standards, and class periods drive instruction. These drivers leave learners little wiggle room to stray from the beaten path.

In 2009, education leaders in southeastern Wisconsin found themselves increasingly frustrated by growing constraints and competing demands. District budgets had shrunk, and schools were stuck in a blender of changing priorities and political discourse. Despite teachers working harder each year, many underperforming students weren't showing the gains they should be showing. Educators throughout the state of Wisconsin were under scrutiny to step things up.

The superintendents in the group considered it a foregone conclusion that there had to be a better way (Rickabaugh, 2016). After a year of study, reflection, and consultation with outside experts, the superintendents decided that the best way forward was to redesign the manner in which their institutions operated. The nexus for any type of redesign had to start with the learner. An immediate call to action secured funding from the regional Cooperative Educational Service Agency #1 (CESA) to establish the Institute for Personalized Learning (IPL). The idea was to form a network of schools to connect, consume, and create a working model for personalized learning.

Since the network's humble beginnings in 2010, Institute membership has grown to more than seventy schools and districts. Robust opportunities for professional development, easy-to-follow toolkits, and cross-pollination of promising practices have allowed participating schools to make significant progress in a relatively short period of time. From the onset, any acceptable design for personalized learning had to meet four criteria:

1. Have the capacity to create a clear path to success for each learner.

2. Be sustainable, without significant increases in staff or work required.

3. Be affordable with current [state and local] resources.

4. Be scalable so that the approach might eventually include entire schools or districts. (Rickabaugh, 2016, pp. ix–x)

Since its inception, the IPL has seen students of all academic and demographic backgrounds benefit from the model. Personalized experiences are underway in urban, suburban, and rural districts of every size and means. Most schools in the network don't have access to outside revenue streams and are working with existing resources to make changes.

PERSPECTIVES FROM THE FIELD

As [students] collaborate and question one another, they fill knowledge gaps better than I could ever imagine possible. They also clear up misconceptions faster and in real time without having to wait for the teacher.

—Kandi Horton, seventh- and eighth-grade personalized learning teacher, Wheatland Center School, Burlington, Wisconsin (ASCD, 2017)

Students in participating IPL districts have experienced growth in unimaginable ways. At Reagan High School in Milwaukee, the graduation rate soared from 73.4 percent to 95.1 percent in the course of five years (Wisconsin Department of Public Instruction, n.d.). In the years prior to implementing personalized learning in Racine Unified School District, Wisconsin—where six out of ten students live in poverty—the district experienced a 7 percent drop in enrollment. Since implementing personalized learning, the number of students leaving for other districts has decreased significantly. Eighty-three percent of Racine teachers report their students are more engaged, and 68 percent of middle school students said their teachers care about them (Education Elements, n.d.).

The IPL has identified three core components to get started on the work, which is graphically represented in a honeycomb design. While it can be tempting to begin with more familiar practices like forming learning groups, deciding on interventions, or purchasing moveable furniture, the Institute cautions against it. Rather, the core components for beginning personalization include the following (Rickabaugh, 2016).

1. **Learner profiles:** Learner profiles provide demographic, academic, aspirational, and other data that paint a detailed picture of each learner. Think of it like customer profiling. Savvy businesses find out as much as they can about their customers to hold onto them and grab new ones. Learner profiles help us build relationships with students, understand things from their perspectives, and improve our return on investment (ROI).

2. **Customized learning paths:** Customized learning paths move schools away from the practice of telling students what their goals should be and focus on working with them to establish goals together. They create short-, intermediate-, and long-term goals jointly. Multiple activities and resources enable each learner to meet his or her goals. Teachers co-determine success markers to measure progress, including the key skills and dispositions that will make learners future-ready. Finally, the teacher and student define how students will demonstrate learning. As students visualize and internalize learning outcomes in advance, the universe of possibilities expands.

3. **Proficiency-based progress:** Progress markers indicate what students will learn, how deep or broad the learning will be, and the exact competencies that teachers will measure. Teachers use standards to articulate clear targets and expected outcomes. Where practical, they give students choices in the sequence of learning, standards-aligned content, and types of assessment that represent proficiency.

As schools chart a course to personalization that works best for their learners, confidence in new practices will escalate. The Learner Profile Template in figure 4.1 offers a gateway to personalization that starts from the lens of the learner. Once we have a picture of each learner's story, we can co-design pathways and outcomes to give students a true sense of purpose in their work.

Before developing a learner profile, talk to students and parents about its purpose. The format of the profile should be such that students and teachers alike can easily

Learner Profile: The Story of	

SCENE 1: Demographic Information	SCENE 2: Academic Information
• About me:	• Test scores:
• About my family:	• Benchmark data:
• About my support team:	• Formative assessments:
• Something I wish my teacher knew:	• Current academic goals:
SCENE 3: Strengths, Interests, and Values	**SCENE 4: Drivers of Learning**
• Things I'm good at:	• I learn best when:
• Things I enjoy doing in my spare time:	• I learn least when:
• Things that matter to me most:	• When I need help, I:
• My hopes for the future:	• I get frustrated when:

Figure 4.1: Learner profile template.

*Visit **go.SolutionTree.com/21stcenturyskills** for a free reproducible version of this figure.*

access, share, and add to it over time. Templates might be in the form of a storyboard, Google Doc, diagram, or drawing depending on the age and grade of the students.

Once you have collated your students' learning profiles and considered the core components necessary for personalization, you can begin to think more deeply about which personalization strategies will work in your classroom, school, or district.

Strategies for Designing Personalized Experiences

This section will present the following strategies teachers and leaders may like to use when designing a personalized learning environment. Educators can:

- Think like a startup
- Shadow a student
- Initiate engagement 2.0
- Pinpoint a student's niche

Think Like a Startup

At what point should students become self-regulated learners? When should educators give up sole ownership of planning, introducing, and assessing curriculum? How much should choice dominate the school day? These questions are at the heart of how we see our role in the learning process. In order to hand over greater control to students, our mindset needs reshaping. The ultimate goal is to allow students to assume more responsibility for what they learn, when they learn it, and how they learn it.

In the corporate world, most breakthroughs come from startups with almost no money, no experience, and few resources. In contrast, business powerhouses with more cash flow, extensive industry knowledge, and high-paid CEOs are often beaten to the punch. Craigslist and eBay forever disrupted the *Penny Saver* and other classified advertisers. Monster and Red Bull have put soft drink giants like Pepsi and Coca-Cola on the ropes. Rideshare companies Uber and Lyft found it easy to overtake the taxi industry as GPS technology winnowed away a cab driver's competitive edge. Airbnb and other online vacation rental sites have pushed hotel chains to step up their game with customer loyalty programs and other incentives. While disruption is not new, many business leaders worry about making the wrong choice. Such worries coupled with an aversion to risk taking lead to strategic paralysis (Leinwand & Mainardi, 2017).

Schools are vulnerable to strategic paralysis too. Our credentials, our experience, and our fear of getting it wrong can blind us to new possibilities. A startup mindset can alter that. The will to act combined with an insatiable desire to give people what they want drives startups to taunt their competitors.

Despite myriad differences between startups and education institutions, one aspect is universal—creativity and customization are team endeavors. Diverse players from all departments and positions put their heads together to generate ideas. Students, like those in the Fallbrook Union Elementary District highlighted in chapter 3, partner with their teachers, principals, and district leaders to enhance their school experience. This lies in stark contrast to the hierarchical structures we see in most schools, where personalization may be viewed at odds with standardization. Both approaches are necessary to build a sustainable learning environment that supports innovation and strengths-based activities within an ecosystem designed to close persistent opportunity gaps. Consider five core philosophies that drive startups (Goryachev, 2018).

1. **Appoint champions:** Internal champions, sometimes called *trailblazers*, are essential when introducing an initiative like personalized learning. In startups, champions influence others, pursue untapped talent, and engage as many people as possible in sharing what a new program or idea has to offer.

2. **Make it a sprint:** Time and again we hear people say, "This is a journey, not a race." But in education, we spend so much time studying, planning, debating, and reflecting that students in our classrooms now rarely benefit from impactful changes. Startups are inspired by a sense of urgency. They use speed to their advantage. In the relatively short school year, the tortoise doesn't have a chance of beating the hare. Slow and steady is only good when we have a lifetime to make something happen.

3. **Pick the right team:** Startups always begin with the best hires. While every teacher has a different set of ideals, priorities, and hot buttons, working together on students' behalf should be a non-negotiable. When looking at teacher transfers or new hires, focus on intangibles like willingness to collaborate, open-mindedness, entrepreneurial spirit, and ability to connect with students. A teacher's internal makeup can add more value than years of experience, content knowledge, or advanced degrees.

4. **Embrace moonshot thinking:** Startups spend the majority of their time focused on what could be instead of what is. They are propelled by *moonshot thinking*—the notion of doing things not because they are easy but because they are hard. Since there's not a lot of past to protect, startups don't have much to lose. *Earthly schools* spend the majority of their time fixating on problems. *Moonshot schools* spend most of their time talking about why and how they'll succeed, no matter how bold an idea may seem. Moonshot educators establish a vision and set goals that push the boundaries of what seems possible.

5. **Create a startup-esque environment:** As startups develop and validate ideas, employees receive support from mentor networks, training, and resources. At one point in time, every school was a startup. Whether a campus is five years old or fifty, we need to recapture that original spark the school had when it first opened. The goal is to stretch team members beyond their regular job duties to create game-changing value for students.

Many organizations that have resisted or failed to embrace market fluctuations and customer preferences are no longer with us. Former household names like Blockbuster, BlackBerry, and Borders have disappeared. Experts argue that public sector institutions risk a similar fate. Pervasive inequalities make schools vulnerable. For example, researchers predict that 825 million children worldwide in low- and middle-income countries (half of today's youth) will reach adulthood without the cognitive and noncognitive skills they need to thrive in work and life (Winthrop, 2018).

If you think inequity is only a third-world phenomenon, think again. Longitudinal data from the National Center for Education Statistics (NCES) indicate that large performance gaps continue to exist in the United States between children in the lowest and highest socioeconomic groups. Low educational achievement leads to fewer economic prospects later in life, representing "a societal failure that betrays the ideal of the 'American dream'" (Garcia & Weiss, 2017, p. 1).

Personalized learning has shown promising results in addressing persistent equity gaps. For example, a RAND study comparing eleven thousand low-income and minority students with nationwide peers noted significant gains in mathematics and reading for students working in personalized learning environments. Within a three-year timespan, students in the personalized settings had scored above average on national assessments (Pane, Steiner, Baird, & Hamilton, 2015). A Stanford University study of personalized learning models in four California high schools found increased graduation rates, greater gains on state achievement tests, higher enrollment in college prep courses, and stronger college persistence rates among the lowest achieving students. Students from all four campuses outperformed peers in neighboring schools with similar populations (Friedlaender, Burns, Lewis-Charp, Cook-Harvey, & Darling-Hammond, 2014).

In schools, there will always be polarities between past practices and startup practices. As such, the best path to personalization should reflect the practices we want students to adopt. If we expect students to collaborate, we must collaborate too. If we want students to question, we must ask. If the point is for students to lead, we must get out of the way. The real power of personalization lies in what we're willing to relinquish, rather than what we insist be retained.

Shadow a Student

Have you ever wondered what it's like for students to go through an entire day in a classroom? Are you intrigued to know more about the impact teachers have on student motivation? Educators have tried different ways to answer these questions. From instructional rounds, to data walks, to Depth of Knowledge (DOK) rubrics, teachers have used various strategies to inform instructional practice. While helpful, these strategies don't provide a true picture of what it's like to be a student. Nor do they reveal the actual conditions under which we expect students to learn. A better way to enlighten practitioners about the need to explore more personalized instructional approaches is through empathy-driven exercises such as Shadow a Student Day.

While serving as superintendent, I wanted to experience firsthand what it felt like to be a student in our schools. Our district was engaged in a number of cutting-edge initiatives and had a strong track record of success. Students graduated with honors and went on to the best colleges and universities. When I visited classrooms, I saw pockets of innovation and customization. However, it seemed like we still had room to grow.

In spring 2016, a principal sent an email inviting every administrator in the district to participate in *Shadow a Student Day*. Our state's professional association was promoting the event that year. Described as a "crash course in empathy that starts with seeing school through students' eyes," Shadow Day has grown to two thousand participants across the United States and fifty-eight other countries (www.shadowa student.org, n.d.). In a nutshell, the experience allows educators to connect the dots among curriculum, instruction, environment, and engagement. Spending an entire day in a student's world—from bus arrival to the final bell—is an authentic way to walk in a learner's shoes.

In my district, five administrators answered the call. Recognizing how it might feel for teachers to have the superintendent in their classroom, I worked with the high school principal (who also participated in the challenge) to coordinate my presence on campus. It was important that teachers didn't object to me being in their classroom or think I was there to evaluate them. I also reached out to a student on my Student-Superintendent Advisory Council to see if I could shadow her. Not only was she delighted to be asked, she took great pride in taking me under her wing.

As I ventured from one seventy-one-minute class to the next, I paid close attention to student-teacher interactions, how teachers delivered instruction, classroom routines, use of resources, and personalized opportunities. I jotted down notes to trigger my memory for later reflection. Most insightful was the play-by-play commentary that my "shadowee" offered. She explained every aspect of teacher expectations, from the proper way to set up my paper for Cornell note taking to using the periodic table during an impromptu chemistry exam. At one point, when a teacher invited students to participate in a think-pair-share, she turned to me and said, "He's never done this before." With the exception of this added flair, the teachers appeared to carry on without any special planning or changes in instructional routines.

After six hours, I returned to my office utterly drained. Despite the delicious salad bar lunch (consumed in thirty-three minutes) and delightful conversations with students, high school was a grueling experience. Except for passing periods (five minutes), there was a lot of sitting. I longed for the freedom of walking around my office chatting with employees, visiting schools, fielding phone calls, driving to Starbucks for a midafternoon passion tea, and laughing. When my secretary asked how it went, I blurted out, "If my job was as confining as the job of being a student, I might have to poke out my eye!"

A week after Shadow Day, those of us who took the challenge got together to debrief. Surprisingly, we all had similar stories. One of the biggest "ahas" was how much administrators and teachers move around all day. This movement keeps us alert and engaged. Even though we're tired at the end of the day, it's a productive kind of tired. Yet, we expect students to sit for long stretches of time with little movement or activity. Block schedules, which are supposed to offer greater depth and flexibility, make passive learning worse. While my fellow shadowers agreed that elementary students had more kinesthetic opportunities than older students, the K–12 experience remains a sit-and-get proposition.

Participation in Shadow Day was a transformative experience. My biggest regret is that I never shadowed students while serving as a principal or teacher. What a difference it might have made in my effectiveness. Walking away from Shadow Day, six takeaways have shaped my views about the road ahead in making school feel more personal and personalized.

1. **High school is really hard:** Despite holding a doctorate, I couldn't pass algebra II or chemistry if my life depended on it. Learning seems to be defined by rigor, while relevance is rarely in the picture.

2. **Students are amazingly compliant:** Although every teacher had a challenging student or two, these students were easily redirected. I wondered how compliant my colleagues and I would be under the same circumstances.

3. **Teacher talk dominates the school day:** Eighty to ninety percent of every class period involved the teacher talking while students passively absorbed the information. Student engagement was either an afterthought or not considered at all.

4. **Students have little autonomy in choosing their learning path:** Well before students entered the classroom, teachers had decided what they'd do, how they'd do it, and how much time they'd have to get it done. All the hype about student voice and choice seems to be a one-sided affair.

5. **The textbook drives the curriculum:** Despite the school being flush with digital resources, the textbook remained the go-to resource for teachers. Class sets of the five-pound books meant students didn't have to haul them around campus, but all the fancy diagrams and glossy photos didn't stimulate a whole lot of interest.

6. **Shadowing should be a requirement for every educator:** The activity could start in teacher prep courses, extend to administrative training programs, and be included in ongoing staff development offerings. School districts could embed reflections on the experience and any subsequent change in practice in their evaluation criteria.

Our blind spots grow over time and limit the way we act, react, and behave. But, of course, we don't know these blind spots exist. The best way to understand the underpinnings of personalized learning is to walk in students' shoes. The outline in figure 4.2 provides a step-by-step sequence to organize a Shadow Day in your school or district. A free toolkit is also available at www.shadowastudent.org with templates and compelling insights from previous shadowers.

Initiate Engagement 2.0

Web 2.0 is a term used to describe the evolution from the original World Wide Web—a static, read-only platform—to a dynamic interface where content and

> **Step 1: Prep**—Create goals for your Shadow Day, select a student, and prepare to question your assumptions.
> **Step 2: Shadow**—Spend an entire day with your student, doing everything he or she does. Capture observations and artifacts in a journal.
> **Step 3: Reflect**—Reflect with a colleague on your observations and artifacts. Question what you discovered. Develop opportunities for action.
> **Step 4: Act**—Based on your Shadow Day findings, create a "hack." A hack is a way to redesign or simplify an element of a school or classroom environment using small experiments. For example, some shadowers are surprised by the number of rules students are expected to follow. Instead of various rules listed everywhere, think, "What is something we can do schoolwide to improve this?"

Source: Shadow a Student Challenge, n.d.

Figure 4.2: Shadow a Student Day preparation and follow-up.

social media came alive (O'Reilly, 2005). Blogs, social media sites, wikis, tagging, video sharing, and hosted services are hallmarks of web 2.0. This new generation of computing turned the internet into a transformational place where every user and industry reassessed their interactions with the world.

Student engagement in schools has evolved in a similar way. Early discussions of student engagement in schools focused primarily on classroom practices and teacher behavior (Skinner & Belmont, 1993). I call this *engagement 1.0*. Following decades of research, academics have identified several factors that promote as well as undermine student engagement. However, most of the literature has focused on influential teacher behaviors such as guidance, modeling, praise, enthusiasm, reinforcement, confidence building, and provisions of choice (Skinner & Belmont, 1993). In essence, claims are that teachers' words and actions underscore a motivation-enhancing classroom. However, without student motivation (such as in engagement 1.0), teachers have no point of entry. Without conditions such as student autonomy, agency, and choice (which we might refer to as engagement 2.0), it's unrealistic to expect much change.

 PERSPECTIVES FROM THE FIELD

Autonomy, as they see it, is different from independence. It's not the rugged, go-it-alone, rely-on-nobody individualism of the American cowboy. It means acting with choice—which means we can be both autonomous and happily interdependent.

—Daniel Pink (2009), *Drive: The Surprising Truth About What Motivates Us*, p. 90

While engagement 1.0 is more about the teacher, engagement 2.0 is where students receive a more influential role in their learning—and it is here that the real magic happens. Engagement 2.0 derives from the EPIC encounters students have with the work they're asked to undertake in schools (see figure 4.3, page 76). Crystallizing experiences occur at the point where attention, interest, and prior success collide. In this environment, the value of learning is evident regardless of extrinsic rewards, teacher pressure, demands for compliance, or fear of failure. As students actively define and discover the purpose of their learning, ownership grows, commitment soars, and outcomes improve (Rickabaugh, 2016). If the only reason to learn something is because "you'll need it next year in sixth grade," "it's on the exam," or "it may come up later," we've lost students forever.

Efficacy: the ability for the encounter to produce a desired or intended result
Perception: the manner in which students see, understand, or interpret the encounter
Involvement: the way students interact with or feel included in the encounter
Choice: the opportunity or power for students to select their direction in the encounter

---

Figure 4.3: EPIC encounters in school.

In the world of engagement 2.0, rigor no longer defines learning. Instead, it's the manner in which students perceive the quality of an opportunity that determines interest and action. Engagement 2.0 is an adventure where students are the main characters and teachers enter their stories with them. Higher levels of engagement happen as students reclaim their space and make informed, uncoerced decisions. Doing something one chooses—rather than what one has been told to do—is the rocket fuel for achievement.

Pinpoint a Student's Niche

Niche. How many times have we heard that word? Probably several. Niche marketing identifies a specific segment of the overall population and devises a plan to meet the preferences and habits of that population. This strategy is especially effective in reaching consumers who share certain characteristics such as age, social or political causes, hobbies, or occupations. For example, businesses consider education a niche market as they try to sell their products to schools. They utilize different strategies to appeal to various segments of the learner population.

To envision how a teacher might employ a niche approach in the classroom, let's first consider how learning blossoms in out-of-class pursuits. Remember *Pokémon GO*? The most hyped mobile game of 2016, *Pokémon GO* features players tracking and collecting characters using their mobile phones. Digital creatures pop up in places around the globe, including the White House lawn. Within seven days of its release, *Pokémon GO*'s popularity exceeded Twitter's 65 million users and crashed servers everywhere. Nintendo, which owns a third of the Pokémon Company, saw its stock prices double (Evans & Anderson, 2016).

Like any craze, *Pokémon GO* has lost its initial luster. But the augmented reality and personalized experiences that hooked players in the first place continue to allow people of all ages to harness the technology they already have in their pockets. As Richardson (2017) explains, "Regardless of their educational path, students moving into adulthood today need more than anything else to be voracious, passionate learners, adept at creating their own personal learning curriculum, finding their own teachers to mentor and guide them in their efforts and connecting with other learners with whom they can collaborate and create" (p. 25). When the compelling aspects of a task (what I do), time (when I do it), technique (how I do it), team (who I do it with), and transferability (how I apply it to other situations) come together, students can't resist. Purposeful activities make for purposeful learning.

The customized playlist in figure 4.4 (page 78) serves as a guide to pinpointing students' niches. While appearing to be a sequential outline, the teacher who created the playlist gives her students the unit plan, including access to all the lessons in text or video form, ahead of time. With the learning plan in hand, students work through the lessons and assignments at their own pace and in the order that suits them best (Gonzalez, 2016).

Playlists also allow teachers to refine their instructional practices by raising questions about where to give students choice, where to have students work independently, where teamwork might come into play, and where data will help redirect the learning path.

Keep in mind a custom playlist isn't a list of options based on what a computer program determines students should be doing (Ferlazzo, 2017). Instead, it's a menu of learning activities in which students decide which activities work best for them. Teachers can modify playlists for any topic or unit of study based on learner needs, interests, performance goals, and academic standards. This example in figure 4.4, from a middle school English class, guides students through the stages of writing an argumentative essay. Notice how the tasks include both technological and nontechnological strategies.

As personalization gains momentum in schools, experts caution educators not to confuse customization with differentiation (Stuart, Heckmann, Mattos, & Buffum, 2018). Differentiation relies on the same primary source—the teacher—to plan and package lessons to appropriately stretch the capabilities of students at varying levels. But the notion that any one teacher can meet the diverse needs in a classroom of thirty-plus students is flawed. Pressure to perform as superheroes perpetuates a cycle of frustration and burnout. Personalization requires that *students* stretch *themselves*. Without opportunities for students to drive their own experiences, niche learning becomes a hit-or-miss proposition.

Conclusion: Settle or Soar

Imagine if the Wright Brothers had given up because Kitty Hawk was too far to reach? What if Michelangelo had refused to paint the Sistine Chapel because he was

Activity	Directions	Notes	Date Completed
1. Review scholarly writing samples.	Choose one of the essays in Google Classroom to read. Complete the Real-World Writing activity sheet.		
2. Examine student essays.	Log into GoFormative and complete the student argument essay sample reflection questions.		
3. View requirements of essay assignment.	Watch the Screencastify video to view actual requirements for your essay or see the teacher in person. Click here for a hard copy assignment.		
4. Choose your topic.	Pick a topic for your essay. Scan these websites for more ideas. Talk to peers if you're having trouble deciding. Once you have an idea, fill out the Topic Go Ahead form. Email or provide a hard copy of the form to the teacher.		
5. Research credible versus noncredible sources.	Watch the YouTube video "How to Know If a Source Is Credible." Take the BrainRush quiz to check your understanding of credible versus noncredible sources.		
6. Select a thesis statement.	Go to https://quizizz.com to learn more about thesis statements. Post your thesis statement on the class Padlet.		
7. Create a graphic organizer.	Once your thesis statement is approved, complete the graphic organizer to start planning the key elements of your essay. Check in with the teacher to discuss.		
8. Draft counterarguments and rebuttals.	Start your first draft. Once you have four to five paragraphs, watch the video link to help write your counterarguments and rebuttals.		
9. Submit a first draft.	Turn in your first draft in Google Classroom.		

Source: Adapted from Gonzalez, 2016.

Figure 4.4: Customized playlist.

a sculptor, not a painter? Where would we be if Marion Donavan had thrown in the towel after paper manufacturers turned down her "superfluous" idea to design a disposable diaper? Luckily, Procter and Gamble saw the value in Marion's vision and turned it into a product called Pampers.

Schools find endless reasons why they can't turn students loose to explore and discover, even though imagination and curiosity are natural outcomes of learning. It's impossible to be curious without the freedom to challenge existing thinking and beliefs. Bringing personalized learning into the mainstream can be rocky if not approached with a discernible structure and clear theory of action. Educators have to understand and internalize the core elements that drive the model to avoid major missteps that breed consternation and resistance.

When students have autonomy to do and be their best, education feels more like a fascination than an obligation. In Steve Jobs's (2005) famous Stanford University commencement address, he told graduates, "The only way to do great work is to love what you do." He implored students not to settle, not to be trapped by dogma—which is the result of other people's thinking—and not to let the noise of others' opinions drown out their own inner voices (Jobs, 2005). Although Jobs was known to be a driver with a big ego, he believed strongly in allowing people to find their niche.

It can be scary to venture outside prevailing norms to transform our practice. As such, our own professional learning has to expand as personalization expands. Action networks like the Institute for Personalized Learning in Wisconsin have shown that collaborating, exchanging resources, and learning from shared experiences allow schools to move forward faster than they would on their own (Rickabaugh, 2016). Any good strategy becomes better when we do it *with* colleagues and students. Schools can either settle on the edge of current practices or soar off that edge. Through supportive communities of practice, educators are learning to ride the winds of personalization together.

In the next chapter, I look at ways to build bridges among internal and external partners that are trying to help the same students. Forming alliances with groups that don't normally work together takes sophistication and an openness that many schools are only beginning to develop. Framed around the notion that excellent schools are everyone's business, chapter 5 introduces sustainable processes to get and keep key stakeholders on your side.

Touchstone Takeaways

Discuss the following Points to Ponder and Rapid-Fire Ideas on your own or within a teacher or leadership team. The questions and activities in this section are designed to shrink the gap between our expectations as educators and students' expectations as learners. When we examine learning through students' eyes, we're in a much better position to approach teaching from a more personalized platform.

Points to Ponder

1. Think back to the best teacher you ever had in school. What did this teacher do that made learning so memorable all these years later?

2. Contemplate the five core philosophies that drive startups. Which philosophies are in play now in your classrooms? What polarities exist between past practices and startup practices? What are you willing to abandon to make learning more personal?

3. Consider this educator's experience after participating in the Shadow a Student Day:

   > I was sitting for 8 hours a day—I am EXHAUSTED. My student was on the Free- and Reduced-Price Lunch program, so I ate what he ate. I had to sneak to the staff room and get a snack in the afternoon—I was starving. It was so hard for me to remain immobile. I asked for a bathroom pass and walked around the hallways instead. (Young, 2016)

   How does this experience compare with a classroom walkthrough you've participated in? What are the potential benefits of shadowing students versus observing students?

4. How might you redesign an upcoming lesson so that students have the autonomy to make informed, uncoerced decisions? What tweaks will guarantee the experience is an EPIC encounter as opposed to simply differentiating tasks?

5. Researchers have used computer recognition software to determine which facial expressions predict learning outcomes (Grafsgaard, Wiggins, Boyer, Wiebe, & Lester, 2013). Students beam engagement from the lower face and eyes. Eyelid tightening and mouth dimpling denote concentration and thinking. I refer to this as "shiny eyes and scrunchy faces." What immediate actions might you take to create a room full of shiny eyes and scrunchy faces? (Hint: Think accessible, relevant, and reflective of how students learn outside school.)

Rapid-Fire Ideas

Consider the following rapid-fire ideas as you begin implementing the ideas from this chapter in your classroom.

Hold a Collaboration Reboot

At your next team meeting, begin a deeper conversation about alignment of personalized learning with existing areas of focus in your school. Use the following three prompts to paint a better picture of current levels of customization in your classrooms.

1. Share a recent academic experience you provided students. Did this experience mimic the type of experience you'd expect to engage in as an adult?

2. What have students learned in the last week that you didn't teach them?

3. What immediate change can we commit to as a team to turn learning from an obligation to a fascination?

Discuss the Fun Factor

On a scale of 1 to 10, rate your level of agreement with this statement: *Learning is fun in my classroom*. Ask students to do the same. Compare ratings. Enlist students' ideas for raising the fun factor. Students who like school because it's *fun* are actually saying it's challenging and worth their time.

Complete the Engagement Meter

The engagement meter (figure 4.5, page 82) offers a quick peek at the elements in your classroom or the classroom of a colleague that make learning more personal. Share your observations and any evidence collected with a colleague. The goal is to focus on what the information may reveal, without judgment or interpretation. Grade-level or department teams can explore ways to redesign activities that will ramp up the five Ts of engagement 2.0.

Engagement Meter

Purpose: This tool focuses attention on what students are doing in the classroom. It's not a teacher evaluation tool; rather, it's intended to measure engagement through the eyes of the learner.

What to expect: Keep in mind not every element will be present every minute of the day. But the more elements in play, the more engaged students will be. As you observe, ask students about what they're doing to get a fuller picture of the impact of each T.

Scoring: 0 = Not Evident (NE); 1 = Partially Evident (PE); 2 = Evident (E); 3 = Strongly Evident (SE)

Five Ts of Engagement 2.0	Learner Behavior	NE (0)	PE (1)	E (2)	SE (3)
Task What students do	Students formulate their own questions and discuss their discoveries.				
	Students extract themes and use their knowledge to solve ill-defined problems.				
Time When and where they do it	Students are given the space to invent, imagine, and test assumptions.				
	Students have time to resolve the unknowns.				
Technique How they do it	Students make choices about how the final product will look.				
	Students take different routes to reach the same destination.				
Team Who they do it with	Students are excited to work with others to complete the task.				
	Students view collaboration as a contributor to their success.				
Transferability Where they'll use it	Students see the value of the task and know why they're doing it.				
	Students improve skills for their own benefit and growth, not to prove something to the teacher.				
Total Score					

Figure 4.5: The engagement meter.

Visit go.SolutionTree.com/21stcenturyskills for a free reproducible version of this figure.

CHAPTER 5

Collaborating With the Outside

The heroic efforts of countless teachers, administrators, and nonprofits, together with billions of dollars in charitable contributions, may have led to important improvements in individual schools and classrooms, yet systemwide progress has seemed virtually unobtainable.
—John Kania and Mark Kramer

In any given week, a school might receive a call to action to expand its breakfast program, develop an early literacy curriculum, or open an after-school tutoring center. Yet, working with external stakeholders to bridge competing demands doesn't come naturally to many educators. The scale and complexity of our system are vast. We worry that outsiders won't or can't fully understand it.

Good schools add immense value to a community—and the public has every right to expect its schools to prepare students for the changing economic times. In *Humanizing the Education Machine*, author Rex Miller and his coauthors (2017) posit that, in a previous era, public education served America well. But with the passing of that era, shifts are necessary to confront outdated education models "just as refrigeration once confronted icehouses and sailing vessels challenged propulsion by oars" (Miller et al., 2017, p. 166). With growing emphasis on post-graduation readiness, access to high-quality learning environments has become an important social justice issue of our time.

Policymakers and pundits alike have expressed frustration that America has fallen behind the rest of the world in its ability to compete educationally. During the Sputnik era, American education received criticism for not being enough like the Soviet Union (Zhao, 2018). After the 1983 publication of *A Nation at Risk* by the National Commission on Excellence in Education, critics denounced American education for not being as tough and rigorous as Japan. In the 1990s, Singapore and

South Korea became the objects of desire. When the first international PISA results came out in 2000, all eyes were on Finland. Growing admiration for education in China is the latest end-all-be-all. Lessons in authority and rigidity are thought to give students a leg up in subjects like computer science, engineering, and mathematics (Zhao, 2018).

In the United States, school reform remains a billion-dollar industry as schools try to fix the "broken" parts of the system (Colvin, 2005). As the money pours in, few schools and districts are unaffected. While America remains hungry for better schools, Yong Zhao (2018) warns that chasing other nations can carry disastrous consequences. The obsession to copy others grows from the simplistic, albeit misguided, view of good test scores as the basis for excellence. Instead of more reforms, schools are better served focusing on collective efforts and a collective journey. This includes active pursuits to get parents, nonprofits, philanthropists, and members of the public on our side.

Hence, this chapter focuses on the fourth touchstone: collaboration with external partners (see figure I.1, page 2). Most schools rely heavily on the donations of parents, local business partners, booster clubs, school foundations, and philanthropic efforts to support a variety of curricular and cocurricular activities. As such, the chapter begins by discussing how outside investors have tried to improve student outcomes and the challenges that come with these partnerships. Next, a successful model known as *collective impact* is introduced to illustrate a structured way schools can work with multiple organizations to bring about hoped-for change. From there, I share strategies to anchor stakeholder engagement around a mission, vision, and graduate profile before delving into ideas to bring work-based learning opportunities into the curriculum. Finally, readers will learn about the expectations of Millennial parents and how to build effective coalitions with all partners to create the best outcomes for students.

Education Philanthropy Through the Ages

Philanthropic organizations focused on helping education have existed for centuries. During the Jim Crow era, the Rosenwald Foundation—one of the earliest foundations in the United States—backed the construction of thousands of schools for African American students (Colvin, 2005). In 1887, automobile heiress Grace Dodge founded Teachers College—now Columbia University. The Ford Foundation was involved in the employment of classroom aides, National Merit Scholarships, and Advanced Placement (AP) testing and curriculum. More recently, the Ford and Rockefeller Foundations joined forces to support equity litigation that dramatically altered how schools are funded in many states (Colvin, 2005).

In the past, wealthy Americans tended to wait until retirement to start giving their money away (Strauss, 2017). However, the ultra-wealthy are making millions at a younger age and want to start their legacy of impact much sooner. Legendary investor Warren Buffett initially thought he would wait until his passing to make his largest donations. But in 2006, Buffett scrapped these plans to give $36.1 billion to the Gates Foundation. Melissa Berman, president of the Rockefeller Philanthropy Advisors, points out that wealthy people engaged in philanthropy strive to be knowledgeable about the issues they care about. Berman notes, "They really want to take a deep dive and spend their time and their energy, as well as their money" (Strauss, 2017).

Table 5.1 highlights some of the high-powered players attempting to raise the bar in contemporary education. Their initiatives reflect a pattern of newfound investment in charter schools, early child development, improved outcomes for students living in poverty, innovation, personalized learning, and college and career readiness.

Table 5.1: High-Powered Players in Education Giving

Foundation	Key Initiatives	Estimated Giving to Education
Walton Family Foundation	• Charter schools and school choice • Building Equity Initiative • Innovation	$1 billion since mid-1990s
The David & Lucile Packard Foundation	• Early childhood development • After-school programs • Teacher coaching	$665 million since 2009
Michael & Susan Dell Foundation	• Quality School Options for students living in urban poverty • Data interoperability	$650 million since 2010
The Eli and Edythe Broad Foundation	• Superintendent leadership • Management and governance • Public charter schools • Teacher quality	$589 million since 1999
Bill & Melinda Gates Foundation	• The College-Ready Promise • Kindergarten readiness • Common Core alignment	Approximately $500 million annually since 2000
Chan Zuckerberg Initiative	• Personalized learning • Customized SAT practice • Literacy	$308 million since 2016

Sources: David & Lucile Packard Foundation, n.d.; Eli & Edythe Broad Foundation, n.d.; Gates & Gates, 2018; GivingCompass, 2018; Informing Change, 2017; Michael & Susan Dell Foundation, 2010; Walton Family Foundation, n.d.

Annual giving in the United States has reached $373 billion, with roughly 19 percent earmarked for education initiatives (Zinsmeister, 2016). Yet, as issues in schooling become more complex, it has grown harder for individual organizations to achieve large-scale change. One reason is that education giving remains highly experimental. Many of the funded initiatives are untested, and little data are collected to measure results. Another reason is a lack of clarity about who's leading the charge. Without understanding who's managing what, the power dynamics can stall momentum and keep well-intended programs from having widespread impact. A third reason is unless public money takes over when private funding goes away, the innovative approaches fizzle out quickly (Colvin, 2005). San Diego Superintendent Cindy Marten—who first served as a principal and teacher in the district—summed up the disconnect this way: "I found way too many people coming into the schools trying to do things to us and trying to do things for us, which is disenfranchising, disempowering and disrespectful of our community. It would always sound good, but that attitude of 'we're going to come and save you' doesn't work. We wanted partners who were thoughtful and relevant around the goals that we were trying to meet" (Grossman, Lombard, & Fisher, 2014). Ultimately, gridlock and bad feelings emerge only to leave a residue of disappointment on all sides. Educators become skeptical of partnerships and are less open to future support. For their part, philanthropists grow impatient waiting for results.

While the education landscape is dotted with a variety of collaborative undertakings, many efforts have shown mixed results. For example, in 2005, the executive director of the Gates Foundation openly acknowledged that ten to twenty percent of the foundation grants weren't working, and another ten to twenty percent were working differently than the foundation had intended (Colvin, 2005). In 2018, high school students in New York took to the streets to protest Summit Learning—an online personalized initiative—supported by the Chan Zuckerberg Initiative (Tate, 2018). Such concerns continued into 2019, with school districts across Kansas and other states dropping the program (Bowles, 2019).

Absent a framework for disparate groups to come together in a structured way, educators and outsiders struggle to work in unison. Sadly, some investors have abandoned their efforts to help schools due to a lack of tangible results. Scholars say that to change the trajectory of partnerships between schools and outside funders, groups have to focus on improved outcomes for students rather than merely convening around a particular initiative or innovative idea (Grossman et al., 2014). When educators and investors come together through a more thoughtful, coordinated approach, it increases the odds that these efforts will move the dial on learning.

The Collective Impact Movement

School-based partnerships, generally within the purview of the principal, tap into outside agencies to play a supportive role. Because site-level staff or parent organizations initiate most partnerships, the sense of ownership can feel one-sided. Additionally, partnerships tend to wane as leadership changes—for example, as a new principal arrives, a new PTA president is elected, a new teacher is asked to coordinate the program, or a new local agency director is hired. Without an infrastructure that supports democratic collaboration, impacts to learning remain superficial at best.

Suppose there was a way to pool resources with other districts, civic organizations, philanthropists, nonprofit groups, and the business community to improve learning? With the imperative for equity front and center, it's impossible for a single teacher, a single school, or a single entity to experience transformative change on its own. Moreover, issues like education, economic stability, housing, and health care are not separate in the lives of families, even though the systems that serve them are. *Catalytic philanthropy* is one way to deal with sustained alignment of education initiatives and regulate the tension between competing interest groups. Catalytic philanthropy provokes educational change through a compelling campaign that creates the conditions for innovation by influencing the behavior of teachers, principals, and other partners involved in the effort.

In 2011, scholars from Stanford University introduced the term *collective impact* to represent a catalytic approach to moving the dial on social change (Kania & Kramer, 2011). The philosophy behind the movement is to create a bridge among competing groups to collaborate on long-term solutions that help the same people. To be effective, collective impact must consider who is engaged, how these entities work together, and how progress happens. The five conditions in table 5.2 provide a framework for carrying out collective impact work in schools.

Table 5.2: Five Conditions of Collective Impact Work

Common Agenda	All participants share a vision for change that includes a common understanding of the problem and a joint approach to solving the problem through agreed-upon actions.
Shared Measurement	All participating organizations agree on the ways they will measure and report success and identify and use a shortlist of common indicators for learning and improvement.
Mutually Reinforcing Activities	A diverse set of stakeholders, across sectors, coordinates a set of differentiated activities through a mutually reinforcing plan of action.
Continuous Communication	All players engage in frequent and structured communication to build trust, ensure mutual objectives, and create common motivation.
Backbone Support	An independently funded staff dedicated to the initiative provides ongoing support by guiding the initiative's vision and strategy, supporting aligned activities, establishing shared measurement practices, building public will, advancing policy, and mobilizing resources.

Source: Kania, Hanley-Brown, & Juster, 2014. Used with permission.

Collective impact is not simply a matter of encouraging more public-private partnerships. Nor does it target short-term solutions, such as providing more reading books for a school library, funding field trips to the local museum, or giving college scholarships. Rather, it is an effort in which multiple organizations coexist through unified action and shared objectives. Supporters of the movement realize that fixing one aspect of student needs (such as affordable after-school daycare, free childhood immunizations, or college and career readiness initiatives) won't make much of a difference unless other parts are improved at the same time (Kania & Kramer, 2011). No matter how innovative, ambitious, or wealthy an organization might be, their money won't enhance learning without the influence of administrators, teachers, and other school stakeholders.

One of the most successful collective impact initiatives to date is the StriveTogether partnership that began in the Cincinnati–Northern Kentucky area in 2006. Over three hundred entities teamed up to improve education around programs that were already in existence (Kania & Kramer, 2011). The initial collaborative pursued a shared agenda with a set of measurable outcomes. A lot of interested, well-meaning people wanted a seat at the table. However, such abundance caused a dilemma. United Way Director Patricia Nagelkirk recalls, "You would sit in these meetings and hear lots of good ideas. But there was no coordinator or game plan to carry them out" (Irby & Boyle, 2014, p. 15).

In greater Cincinnati, corporate CEOs, government officials, school superintendents, and college presidents joined forces with dozens of education nonprofits and agreed that unless they could improve all parts of the system together, long-term change would remain wishful thinking. Skipping meetings or sending lower-level surrogates to represent the organization was unacceptable. Group leaders didn't want *collective impact* to become the new buzzword for *collaboration of all types*. Nor did they want partners to merely write a check.

To that end, the group established Student Success Networks (SSNs) where individual partners could work in areas they were most passionate about. Network categories included *Prepare for School, Support In and Out of School, Succeed Academically, Enroll in College,* and *Enter a Career.* Over time, StriveTogether introduced benchmarks and data collection requirements. It required each Student Success Network to meet with facilitators for two hours every two weeks to develop shared performance indicators, discuss progress, learn from one another, and align resources (Kania & Kramer, 2011).

Within four years of StriveTogether's inception, thirty-four of the fifty-three success indicators had trended upward (Kania & Kramer, 2011). Partner collaboration had improved results across three large public school districts in key areas such as increased graduation rates, fourth-grade reading and mathematics scores, and the number of children prepared for kindergarten.

PERSPECTIVES FROM THE FIELD

Just having business leaders show up was valuable. They brought a fresh approach and asked the . . . questions that needed to be asked to move the conversation beyond typical education-speak.

—Jeff Edmondson, founding director, StriveTogether (Grossman et al., 2014, page 3)

Today, StriveTogether reaches 10.4 million students via a national network of seventy community partnerships across thirty states and the District of Columbia. Strive's ambitious mission is to coordinate improvements from cradle to career. Collaboration is tied to six outcomes: (1) kindergarten readiness, (2) early grade reading, (3) middle-grade mathematics, (4) high school graduation, (5) postsecondary enrollment, and (6) postsecondary completion. After a decade of cross-sector integration, nearly 80 percent of Strive's key indicators are improving (www.strive together.org). Releasing baseline report cards to the community and maintaining an infrastructure to support a partnership's daily management are essential to network participation (Grossman et al., 2014).

Anchoring Engagement Around a Shared Mission, Vision, and Graduate Profile

Strong mission and vision statements can anchor collective impact work in schools and help external partnerships thrive. Not only do these statements solidify common goals, they allow stakeholders to see students' future through a shared lens. Effective schools and school districts develop mission and vision statements that embody the latest thinking about teaching and learning. In fact, a key responsibility of education leaders is to ensure their organization has current and compelling mission and vision statements that drive their work.

A good mission statement makes clear the reason your school or district exists. It reflects the organization's primary purpose and overall intentions. A mission statement is the *what*. In our most successful schools and districts, educating students is the heartbeat of our mission. A vision statement, on the other hand, sets forth a description of the future a school or district aspires to create; it's the *why*. Vision statements define an optimal state that's bursting with possibilities. These statements project hope and energy.

I've had the privilege of working with some forward-thinking school districts to refresh their mission and vision statements through a community-based process. For example, in 2017, the Del Mar Union School District in north San Diego County set out to make education look "radically different" through a process called District

Design 2022 (Billing, 2017). A district design team made up of teachers, principals, school board members, central office administrators, industry experts, university educators, civic leaders, and parents met over the course of three months to ensure students remained energized and engaged throughout their K–6 experience. At the time, Superintendent Holly McClurg told the design team, "The district will always focus on academic instruction, on creating great writers, readers, and fearless mathematicians. But we also know from everything we've researched over the last four years that children need a school experience that is different from the traditional model" (Billing, 2017, p. 2).

Through a series of workshops, the district design team established a new vision statement and priority actions to move forward. The new vision statement *Unrelenting Pursuit of the Extraordinary School Experience* led to the development of three areas of focus: (1) strong academic core and high-quality instruction; (2) skills that matter most; and (3) learning environment. The team identified specific objectives within each focus area to connect teacher and principal actions with student performance over the next five years. (To learn more about Del Mar's progress in its District Design 2022 plan, visit www.dmusd.org.)

When was the last time your school refreshed its mission and vision statements? At the school level, a good rule of thumb is to revisit these statements every four years or whenever a new principal arrives. At the district level, educators should look at these statements every three years or whenever a new superintendent or school board member joins the district. If your district already has compelling (and current) vision and mission statements, unique statements for each school aren't necessary. However, if a school does have separate mission and vision statements, it should be in direct alignment with the district's mission and vision statements. Use the following questions to determine if a refresh is in order.

- Do the mission and vision statements establish context that give meaning to human activity?

- Are they short, coherent, and memorable?

- Are the statements free from methods, means, and how-tos?

- Do the statements guide the school or district's plans, strategies, and actions?

- Do the statements project the value of education to stakeholders (students, parents, and the community at large)?

Not every organization has both a mission and vision statement. It's a personal preference. What is important is that these statements inspire the people who work in the organization and help establish priorities and set direction for the year. (See Sample District Exemplars in figure 5.1.) When employees can recite a vision or mission statement from memory, it's a good sign that these statements mean something to people.

Mission Statements	Vision Statements
We provide every student an extraordinary education in an inspiring environment (11 words)	Igniting passion in today's students for tomorrow's opportunities (8 words)
To ignite genius and empower students to advance the world (10 words)	Unrelenting pursuit of the extraordinary school experience (7 words)
To provide a personalized learning environment, with caring staff (9 words)	Happy students, in healthy relationships, on a path to gainful employment (11 words)
We give students the tools to find their passion and make their way in life (15 words)	Illuminating a path to future-ready learning and citizenship (9 words)

Figure 5.1: Sample district exemplars.

To build coherence around mission and vision statements, districts should also articulate a profile of cognitive and interpersonal competencies that reflect what all students should have when they leave the K–12 system. Referred to as a *graduate profile*, this document brings to life the *what* of students' school experience (see the appendix, page 109).

Designing a graduate profile is not a new concept. What is new is a growing movement to create a portrait of a future-ready learner with input from internal and external stakeholders. Some districts are incorporating the development of a graduate profile within the context of refreshing their mission or vision statements. Other districts have established a separate focus group with broad-based staff and community membership to paint a picture of a future-ready learner.

Unlike a mission or vision statement, a graduate profile is a document that is used to highlight students' interpersonal competencies that fall outside the realm of academics. These competencies can support collective impact initiatives in three ways. First and foremost, a graduate profile helps school districts and donors direct resources toward core dispositions that the state standards don't explicitly address. Second, it provides a clear visualization of priority goals that teachers can succinctly convey to students, parents, staff, and the greater community. Third, it establishes agreed-upon competencies across grade levels, subject areas, and disciplines to align a district's mission, vision, and collective efforts. As we think about our own strategic work, a graduate profile is something to inspire and guide us. Similar to the proposed timelines for refreshing mission and vision statements, a graduate profile should be reviewed and updated as needed every three to five years.

Recent workforce readiness reports affirm the need for schools to think in terms of graduate profile competencies. For example, the National Association of Colleges and Employers job outlook survey lists problem solving and the ability to work in teams as top priorities, with written communication, leadership, and work ethic coming in a close second (Healy, 2018). The Pew Research Center's *The Future of Jobs and Job Training* guide identifies "soft" and "human" skills as crucial employability factors in the labor force of the future (Healy, 2018). Soft and human skills like teamwork, empathy, and persistence combine social-emotional intelligence with communication, temperament, and character to perform well with others. Finally, Deloitte's *Global Human Capital Trends* highlights the growing demand for increased collaboration and internal integration to shape an organization's purpose, guide its relationships with stakeholders, help it act transparently, and influence its ultimate success or failure (Agarwal et al., 2018). School and district leadership should consult such workforce readiness reports when creating their graduate profiles.

Some school districts may try to settle on a graduate profile that is twenty items deep. However, a laundry list will only dilute the document's importance. A reasonable number of core competencies (ideally six to eight) is desirable. It may be hard to imagine turning a kindergartner into an agile, resilient adult, but cultivating these vital dispositions early ensures students are prepared and marketable by the time they leave high school. Whether we work at the elementary or secondary level, our focus should be on leading learning beyond the textbook to prepare students for the modern world.

Opening Doors to Work-Based Learning

For students, it's hard to know what kind of career to pursue without exposure to certain fields and professions. For businesses, it's challenging to ensure prospective employees acquire the knowledge and dispositions aligned with workforce needs. For teachers, it's difficult to present authentic on-the-job experiences through traditional curriculum delivery methods. For parents, it's overwhelming to try to help youngsters navigate job options that fit their passions. Opening doors through work-based learning is a growing trend that can help address these gaps on all fronts. Experiences involve student interactions with industry experts that are linked to school-based instruction. Interactions might include internships, job shadowing, mentoring, virtual experiences, guest panels, and industry-driven projects. Teachers intentionally design these relationships to extend and deepen classroom learning toward real-world outcomes.

A continuum of work-based learning experiences stretching from kindergarten into adulthood is necessary for students to become fully immersed in a field of interest by the time they leave high school (see figure 5.2). Through direct interaction with professionals who are working in the field, work-based experiences enable students to learn *about* work, *through* work, and *for* work.

For work-based learning experiences to become a primary instructional strategy, educators must drive experiences by student outcomes, not activities. Such outcomes should focus on agreed-upon college and career readiness indicators. Factors like schedules, availability of industry partners, teacher preference, and ad hoc events cannot dictate the work.

Student Work-Based Learning Continuum

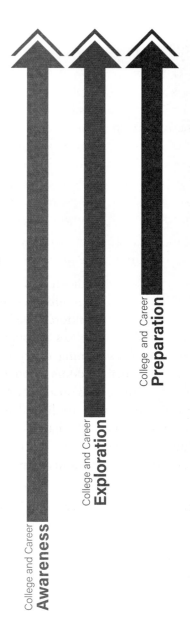

College and Career **Awareness**

College and Career **Exploration**

College and Career **Preparation**

Learning **ABOUT** College and Career	Learning **ABOUT** College and Career	Learning **THROUGH** College and Career	Learning **THROUGH** College and Career
Goal: Build awareness of the variety of careers available.	**Goal:** Explore career options and make a decision.	**Goal:** Apply learning through practical experience.	**Goal:** Build skill and ability for employment.
Experience is defined by: • One-time interaction with partners, often for a group of students	**Experience is defined by:** • One-time interaction with partners for a single student or small group	**Experience is defined by:** • Direct interaction with partners over extended period of time for a single student	**Experience is defined by:** • Direct interaction with partners over extended period of time for a single student
Activities can include: • Workplace tour • Guest speaker • Career fair • Visit parent or guardian at work.	**Activities can include:** • Informational interview • Job shadow • Virtual exchange with a partner • Mock interview	**Activities can include:** • Industry-driven project • Student-run enterprise • Virtual experience • Internship connected to curriculum	**Activities can include:** • Industry-driven project • Student-run enterprise • Virtual experience • Internship connected to curriculum

Source: San Diego County Office of Education, n.d. Used with permission.

Figure 5.2: Work-based learning continuum.

Connecting classrooms to workforce professionals is a signature practice of any career readiness endeavor. To that end, a consortium of fourteen school districts (mine included) and five community colleges in San Diego County received a $13 million grant in 2015 from the California Department of Education to build a career development program that focused on robust employer engagement. The consortium concentrated the program around three major growth sectors in San Diego: (1) advanced manufacturing, (2) clean energy, and (3) information and communication technology.

One of the most compelling features of the grant was an *e*portal that offered everything from managing staff development resources, to linking businesses, nonprofit groups, students, and educators, to offering work-based learning opportunities. As the lead superintendent in the consortium, I heard concerns from business leaders like Qualcomm, Cox Communications, and NRG about the haphazard way partnerships formed with schools. Individual teachers, principals, and school foundations inundated companies with daily requests for support. Yet, there was no centralized mechanism to track requests, evaluate needs, or align resources with corporate goals.

In 2016, the San Diego County Office of Education launched a user-friendly website to facilitate work-based learning experiences through a range of integrated services. (You can view the platform at https://www.sdcoe.net/innovation/cte/Pages /WBL.aspx; San Diego County Office of Education, n.d.) Not only does this *e*portal expose students to the wide array of occupations that make up the regional labor market, it pushes young people to envision their future careers while still in school. Job shadowing, career coaching networks, and online mentoring discussion boards help develop talent that then fills entry- and middle-level positions throughout San Diego County. One of the signature features of the *e*portal is the ability to track users (employers, teachers, and students) and follow students to see how curriculum is influencing their occupational experiences. The *e*portal is supporting business-education partnerships in ways never thought possible.

The collaboration underway in the San Diego region has been groundbreaking for educators as well as industry partners. The added bonus of the *e*portal gives companies a venue to communicate hiring needs to the education sector to ensure students are available to meet their most in-demand requirements. Although curriculum, classroom activities, and school projects offer students a cursory understanding of career opportunities, it is these firsthand interactions that provide authentic experiences for learners to understand what it truly means to have a career.

Collaborating With Millennial Parents

We don't need another study to tell us the value of parent support. Positive parent-teacher relationships provide the foundation upon which families build to get involved with their child's education. Parental involvement remains a strong predictor of higher academic achievement, regular attendance, better behavior, and enhanced social skills even for high school students (Lawson & Lawson, 2012; Patrikakou, 2008). The more we can integrate parents into the learning environment, the better off our students will be.

Each generation of parents develops its own signature parenting style. So what's notable about Millennial parents—those born roughly between 1981 and 2000 (Lovely & Buffum, 2007)? And how do their views about schooling differ from their own parents' views? First, Millennials are having children later in life. By the time their firstborn enters kindergarten, most are in their thirties (Greenthal, 2018). The significance for educators is that Millennial parents tend to be better informed and more experienced than their Baby Boomer parents were. They want meaningful academic programs, personalized learning options, extracurricular activities, and strong teacher-student relationships (Young, 2016).

Another parental shift is that the "helicopter" style, which became a trademark of Baby Boomer parents, is less intense (Steinmetz, 2015). While Millennials are still very involved in their children's lives, they tend to follow and respond rather than direct and schedule. Acting more like drones, Millennials remember the pressure they felt as their parents hovered in the classroom, on the soccer field, and at the school dance. With smartphones, tablets, and apps now readily available, Millennials prefer to collect data and track their children's moves from afar.

A third parental shift is the way Millennials learn to be better parents. Unlike Baby Boomers, who relied on Dr. Spock for advice, Millennials seek out experts in every field through virtual and real contacts (Greenthal, 2018). Over two-thirds tap into social media for advice from raising an autistic child to picking out a college. Bound by a sense of honesty and shared experiences, "mommy bloggers" chronicle the trials and tribulations of parenthood. In these public diaries, Millennial parents rate their children's teachers, outline the right questions to ask at a parent conference, brag about grades, and reveal their frustrations arising out of an IEP meeting—all in the same week. Their openness and candor can catch unprepared educators off guard.

Millennial parents have the sophistication to sift through new ideas that will make their children well-rounded learners. They want their daughters to be scientists and their sons to be in the school play. They're willing to accept teachers' opinions, as long as these opinions help their student advance in ways that prepare him or her for success in life. Five tips can help educators win over today's parents.

1. **Actively communicate:** When communicating, think sound bites and tweets, texts over email. Create a class website or parent portal with details on homework, long-term projects, and a place to respond to parent questions. Resources should be pertinent to the activities of the moment. Be specific about how parents can support learning at home. Generic suggestions like "read to your child each night" won't cut it. Millennial parents want deliberate, intentional direction on how to help their child reach new levels of satisfaction and success.

2. **Recognize their contributions:** Raised under a spotlight of perfection, Millennials may feel fierce pressure to be "perfect parents." Social media can turn joy into guilt when parents see a picture of the magnificent robotics project their child's classmate has turned in. Millennials need affirmation that their parenting is on track. For continuous relationship building, acknowledge parents' contributions regardless of the circumstances.

3. **Consider the modern family:** Married couples comprise only 68 percent of parents today, compared to 93 percent in the 1950s (Greenthal, 2018). Blended families, single parents, multiracial parents, and same-sex couples are all raising children. Grandparents are also an important part of the equation. Pay attention to family dynamics, including any struggles parents may be facing. The first thing children universally participate in that's bigger than their family is an elementary classroom. The goal is to ensure youngsters flourish in an atmosphere of compassion and inclusivity.

4. **Customize learning:** Millennial parents understand a school's obligation to keep up with the curriculum, meet the standards, and make sure every student is career or college ready. However, they grow tired of hearing that teachers have thirty-plus students in the class, with limited time for exploration and creativity. What distinguishes Millennial parenting from previous generations is a belief that learning should be customized. Parents want teachers to treat their children as customers rather than compulsory attendees. The more educators tap into students' unique interests and aspirations, the more impressed their parents will be.

5. **Minimize the need for public venting:** Crowdsourcing and peer solidarity are part of the Millennial DNA. Connectivity to college roommates, neighbors, friends, relatives, and outside sources of information is just a click away. The notion of waiting to address an issue at a parent-teacher conference or remaining silent when a situation erupts at school is a recipe for disaster. To avoid a social media tsunami, reach out early and often. Those who tell first are usually believed.

Connecting with Millennial parents is an emergent, ongoing process. This generation leads highly pressured lives as they try to make ends meet and juggle an array of family demands. Empathy and flexibility are imperative as parents try to renegotiate deadlines or seek accommodations. After all, they don't want to miss important school events or be excluded from special activities. Rather than defaulting to "no," find ways to say "yes." Parental expectations are part of our social milieu and provide the foundation for relationship-based engagement (see figure 5.3).

In the not-too-distant past, parents assumed an ancillary role to educators. This isn't the case today. In addition to the shifting roles of parents is the ever-present scrutiny of social media, where parents freely share their experiences with the world. We can't allow our expectations of parents to shape our frustrations or define how we interact with them. A new type of connectedness is necessary to meet in the middle so that we grow stronger and better together.

> **Choices:** "We'll go elsewhere if our children aren't happy."
> **Being Heard:** "Treat our ideas and input respectfully."
> **Transparency:** "Don't promise what you can't deliver."
> **Inclusion:** "We want 'in' on the whole picture."
> **Tolerance:** "We have zero tolerance for intolerance."

Figure 5.3: What Millennial parents expect from schools.

Building Effective Coalitions

Every school, every city, every church, every nonprofit, and every social service agency has a distinct way of doing things. Organizational culture eminently influences the values, behavior, and myriad decisions of any collaborative effort. Silos can stall progress and derail our work with constituents. Therefore, when we invite people to the table who look and see the world differently than us, we have to put our own agendas aside. Three Es can draw and hold team members together (Lovely, 2017).

1. **Explore:** Find out which agencies in your community or region are interested in supporting your school or district and learn what goals they have for their funds. Understand the assets that they bring to the table that you don't have. Determine how these assets complement your existing programs or fill a specific student or family need.

2. **Enroll:** While numerous businesses and nonprofits may want to help education, don't assume they will automatically include your school or district in the equation. Donors have to be convinced that their time, energy, and resources are more important for your students than someone else's. To enroll partners in your cause, develop a compelling story. Invite prospective grantees to participate in key activities or events. Involve students in the "enrollment" process. When outside players make an emotional connection to your work, they're more eager to get involved.

3. **Engage:** Don't leave important internal partners such as teachers, parent-teacher organizations, school foundations, and booster clubs out of the loop. Engaging and including internal stakeholders is vital to the success of any external endeavor. If internal stakeholders feel excluded or overlooked, it can lead to turf wars and bruised egos.

Educators need external and internal stakeholders on their side to support future-ready schools. A stakeholder is anyone who can affect or is affected by the welfare of the school or its students. In a word, it's anyone who has a "stake" in what goes on inside the building (Great Schools Partnership, 2014). External stakeholders might include the local Boys and Girls Club who welcomes students after school for free tutoring, the retirement community down the street who is affected by school traffic and noise, the local police and fire departments who stand ready to respond to a threat or emergency, and local businesses who employ parents or give generously to school programs. Internal stakeholders include teachers, staff members, union leaders, parents, PTAs or PTOs, booster clubs, and foundations. It's important to know who these important stakeholders are and what level of influence and dependence they have on your organization. Giving voice to stakeholder ideas and perspectives builds effective coalitions. It's imperative that we capitalize on these intrinsic assets to enhance learning opportunities for our students.

The Sandbox Manifesto

Existing collaborations between industry and schools include many promising practices as described throughout the chapter. However, forming alliances with people who aren't accustomed to playing in the same sandbox, so to speak, requires new rules and tools. Well-intentioned, external groups can be driven by self-interests. This can raise suspicions about the motives of outsiders.

The sandbox is a place where we learn the value of play and the value of people. Everyone has a lot more fun when a sense of trust and fairness prevails. Exuberance isn't determined by how hard we play, but instead by how nicely we play together in this small space.

To work better and stronger with external stakeholders, consider the following six tenets of the Sandbox Manifesto (Kania, Hanleybrown, & Juster, 2014).

1. **Get the right people in the room:** Industry experts and those with lived experiences (students, teachers, and administrators) have to understand and address challenges together. Before forming any type of coalition, make sure the right people are in the room. Everyone must agree on the issues they're addressing before they proceed.

2. **Treat relationships as importantly as the rationale:** A lack of personal relationships overshadowed by the presence of strong opinions and difficult historical interactions can impede efforts. If people don't put relationships first, no matter how good the rationale for the work might be, things will deteriorate quickly.

3. **Share credit:** Nonprofits often feel pressure from their donors and boards to demonstrate their unique impact to receive grant funding. But the individual desires of one group to seek or take credit for its work over another can be a barrier to progress. In any venture, sharing credit is far more powerful than taking it. Draw attention to contributions through joint communiqués and mutually reinforcing activities.

4. **Look at existing assets:** Be sure to honor the great ideas and programs that are already in place in your school or district. If organizations ignore existing assets, people will think the answers come by bringing in something new. Moreover, collaboration afflicted with "programitis" can become draining on all sides. While administrators may introduce new programs with the best of intentions, these programs can trap schools in a cycle of

consumption. Use the Initiative Inventory in figure 2.1 (page 28) to help bring focus to the work.

5. **Use structure over strategy:** To build momentum, participants have to collectively see, learn, and do together. While it's tempting to want to create a tangible set of activities to solve a problem, it's more important to determine how stakeholders will engage with each other. Norms and commitments provide conformity to group behavior and bring understanding to what is and isn't working. When strategy precedes structure, there is no foundation on which to frame efforts and conduct.

6. **Avoid silver bullets:** Silver bullet approaches can be enticing, but are full of hidden dangers. Easy fixes won't solve messy problems. In fact, coalitions are more apt to achieve project success through a multitude of unimpressive, small solutions rather than a single one aimed at one cause.

There are numerous reasons why businesses and outside agencies should engage with schools. However, without new rules and tools about who specifically is engaged, how people work together, and how progress happens, the sandbox will be dotted with stumbling blocks. Even in the best of circumstances, group dynamics can be dicey. Changing our approach to external collaboration has significant implications for how educators implement initiatives, how funders incentivize and collaborate with schools, and how policymakers attempt to mandate widespread solutions.

Conclusion: Lower the Drawbridge

Public education belongs to the public. In general, Americans still have faith in our educational institutions and continue to see schools as the cornerstone of democracy. However, citizens expect schools to be accountable, effective, and successful with all students.

Today's reality is simple. Parents shop for their children's education the same way they shop for other important family purchases. Consumers are willing to sacrifice certain things and pay more for a home to live in a good school district. Research has consistently shown that the quality of local schools impacts business relocation and expansion decisions as well (Stoops, 2018). Since we sell education, it's essential to know how to package it, describe it, guarantee it, and seek support for it.

When a community cares about its schools, schools perform better. Additionally, community support is a universal characteristic of high-performing schools. Yet, most involvement remains at a distance from the heart of our school and district missions. Without mutually reinforcing engagement, sweeping improvements are hit or miss.

Business leaders, philanthropists, parents, and educators all recognize that preparing future-ready learners is not a one-sided affair. Education is no longer about learning the curriculum; it's about where the curriculum will take our learners. For schools to function as the great equalizer for society, educators must lower the drawbridge and open the gates to the outside community.

Touchstone Takeaways

Discuss the following Points to Ponder and Rapid-Fire Ideas on your own or within a teacher or leadership team. The questions and follow-up exercises in this section are designed to enhance collaborative efforts with external and internal stakeholders and make informed decisions surrounding collective impact work.

Points to Ponder

1. Consider the different benefits of a graduate profile. How might you introduce core dispositions into your curriculum? What measurements could you use to meaningfully differentiate success or effectiveness?

2. Review the Work-Based Learning Continuum in figure 5.2 (page 93). Compile a list of the college and career awareness, exploration, and preparation endeavors that are underway in your school or district. How might you broaden these experiences to open more doors to the world of work?

3. Developing sensitivity toward Millennial parents requires an understanding of how our own generational makeup—whether we're Millennials, Gen Xers, or Baby Boomers—affects our perspective. What assumptions do you make about parental demands? What two to three actions can you take to walk in parents' shoes and breed more harmony between home and school?

4. Contemplate any collective impact initiatives that have taken shape or matured in your school or district. Use these questions to evaluate efforts.

   • How are relationships developing (or have they developed) among external partners?

   • What do you see as progress?

   • What factors are limiting progress? How can you address these factors?

   • What differences do you notice in learning outcomes as a result of this work?

   • What ripple effect is this work having on other parts of your organization?

5. What judgments do you make about external stakeholder groups, especially when their expectations don't match your own? How might you shift your thinking to forge better partnerships?

Rapid-Fire Ideas

Consider the following rapid-fire ideas as you begin implementing the ideas from this chapter in your classroom.

Create a Graduate Profile

Assemble an advisory group that consists of teachers, parents, administrators, business leaders, and voices from the broader community. For middle and high schools, consider including students on the committee. Share samples of the graduate profiles included in the appendix (page 109) to give members a conceptual framework of what one looks like. Discuss how a graduate profile differs from mission and vision statements. Put participants into mixed teams to answer the following questions.

- What hopes, aspirations, and dreams does our community have for its young people?

- Which dispositions or habits of mind do our students need for success in the rapidly changing, complex world?

- Which dispositions or habits of mind will give our students a competitive advantage in the "any collar" workforce (see page 12)?

Once groups record their ideas, look for common themes. Try to reach agreement on six to eight core dispositions that articulate a collective vision of the community's aspirations for all learners. Form a subcommittee to draft descriptors for each disposition. Solicit refinements from the entire group through a shared Google Doc. Once you have reached consensus on the final dispositions and descriptors, promote the graduate profile for adoption by your school site council, leadership team, or board of education.

Assess Soft Skills

To take skill development to the next level, tools are necessary to evaluate "soft skills". While vendors are pitching a variety of instruments for purchase under the Every Student Succeeds Act (ESSA; 2015), districts may be better served designing their own tools in this new frontier of education measurement. Critical to the process is a commitment that the school will *not* use any "soft skill" measurement for high-stakes evaluation, such as a teacher determining that a student is in the 80th percentile in resiliency or ranks in the bottom quartile on the collaboration spectrum. The minute this occurs, the entire point of the exercise becomes counterproductive.

The following tool (figure 5.4, page 102) can help educators assess growth, design learning goals, and align curriculum with industry needs. Note that the items on this rubric are for the purpose of creating a working example. Schools can add or substitute items to fit their needs.

At the beginning of each quarter, grade-level or department teams should identify a unit of study, a group- or project-based learning activity, and a handful of classroom assignments in which they will conduct thoughtful assessments of soft skill development. Teachers can average scores and discuss them with students as they complete each exercise. Teachers can also share cumulative growth, progress, and future goals with parents in report cards.

Scoring Guide: Use the rating scale 1 (Emerging), 2 (Developing), 3 (Accomplished), and 4 (Exemplary) to assess students' strengths and gaps in the following dispositions. The idea is to gather and track observable data to inform teaching practice and provide useful feedback to students, parents, and the community.

Category	Core Dispositions	Score (1 to 4)	Notes and Observations
Self-Management Measures how well a student is able to take control over what otherwise might be automatic responses	• Adaptable • Agile • Flexible • Resilient	_____ _____ _____ _____	
Social Skills Measures how well a student interacts with peers	• Collaborator • Contributor • Leader • Open-minded	_____ _____ _____ _____	
Academic Achievement Measures cognitive functions that help students carry out academic tasks	• Curiosity • Critical thinker • Problem finder and solver • Initiative • Communication	_____ _____ _____ _____ _____	

Source: Adapted from Whitehurst, 2016.

Figure 5.4: Soft skills assessment.

*Visit **go.SolutionTree.com/21stcenturyskills** for a free reproducible version of this figure.*

Welcome Outside Voices

Invite industry experts to speak to staff about their thoughts on education and how they see students' preparation for the workforce of the future. Bring a panel of high school seniors in to hear their perspectives from the classroom. Have them share how your school has prepared them for graduation. As students contemplate what lies ahead (college, the military, technical career, the big world), ask what they wish they had learned or experienced in elementary, middle, or high school that might have helped them feel more prepared.

Design a Job Posting

Invite representatives from local businesses to speak to students about their business models, hiring practices, and cultural nuances. Ask students to design a job posting that reflects the "soft skills" that align with these employers' needs. As an extension, students can submit a resume and letter of interest to the company as a prospective job applicant.

Consider Models Worth Emulating

At your next staff meeting, discuss collective impact efforts in your community or region that may be worth emulating. What models seem to enjoy the most success and why? Make a list of influential foundations, advocacy groups, corporations, or nonprofits with which an alliance might benefit students. Enlist volunteers to serve on a committee with the principal to pursue one or two new alliances. Clarify lines of communication and accountability to ensure partner-school alignment enhances an existing school program or helps launch a new one.

Epilogue

"I can't wait to get home to look at the district's website."

—Nobody

Like it or not, schools no longer have a monopoly on the teaching and learning marketplace. No one is sitting at home waiting for your website to be updated to learn about the exciting things happening in your workplace. Without a differentiated presence that attracts and holds on to a loyal following, educators may find themselves out in the cold. It's no longer enough to sell an "excellent education." We must also deliver on our promise.

Educators cannot simply coast along doing what we've always done. Innovation, strengths-based education, personalized experiences, and external collaboration are rallying points for future-focused teaching and learning. Technology, lifestyles, politics, family dynamics, and economic drivers have outgrown the industrial era in which our public schools were originally designed. Excellent schools are everyone's business. Therefore, our mission is to develop learning opportunities today that parallel how students will spend their lives tomorrow.

Assess Your Identity

The implications for how schools operate and for what our students need to know and do when they leave the K–12 system are significant. Why do we educate people? How do we ensure our schools remain relevant? How do we convince parents, politicians, and the community-at-large that the students we teach will be ready for anything? Today's consumers are smarter, hipper, and more skeptical of public institutions than in the past. What others think about us matters.

Strengthening education's value to the outside world requires a message that resonates with a broad audience. This takes time and soul searching. But, when done right, schools build trust and confidence into the work they are doing. A good message is easy to spot; it tells the story of your organization and the core values that drive the work. Amazon CEO Jeff Bezos coined the phrase, "Your brand is what other people say about you when you leave the room" (Arruda, 2016). If everyone who interfaces with the programs, services, and opportunities you offer students reinforces a compelling message about your school, the rewards of branding will be reaped.

To assess your organization's identity, consider what students say about you when you're not in the room. Or, more importantly, what do they say when they've been out of your class for ten years? What do parents say at the swim meet or the grocery store? What does the mayor say when she's talking to local business leaders about the schools in her city? What does the police chief say after his officers respond to a school safety threat? What do religious leaders tell their congregations about the campuses in their neighborhood? Don't think for a minute that reputation management is simply the job of the principal, superintendent, or district public information officer. Every teacher, counselor, staff member, and administrator in your system is a brand ambassador.

Educators are great at talking about curriculum, unpacking standards, looking at test data, and identifying students who are slipping through the cracks. But when was the last time your team assessed its messaging? Shaping perceptions that advance a school or district's mission and vision starts with staff awareness followed by intentional action. Effective branding helps people make an emotional connection to your work.

Figure E.1 depicts three elements of a compelling message. The goal is to determine how well your practices are keeping up with the times and if your organization is producing the outcomes parents and the community expect.

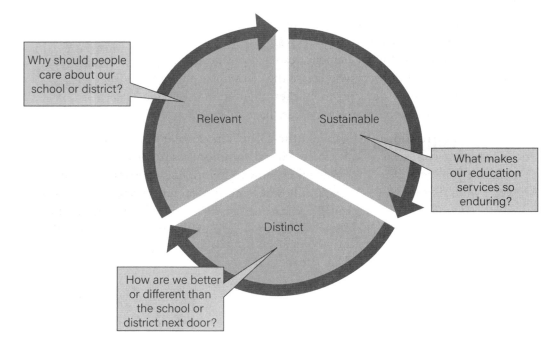

Figure E.1: Three elements of a compelling message.

Turn Words Into a Movement

Conversations are a tradition as old as time. It's how we exchange knowledge, let others know what we care about, solve problems, and contemplate the future. Educators have successfully engaged in conversations that deal with hard questions. But how do we turn our words into a movement? We've all been witness to (or perhaps been a part of) political and social movements that have altered the course of history. In the 1960s, the civil rights movement gave African Americans equal opportunities and rights of citizenship guaranteed in the Constitution. In the 1970s, the anti-war movement helped put an end to the Vietnam War. In the 1980s and 1990s, we saw freedom movements bring down the Berlin Wall, end apartheid, and shift the political culture in China. More recently Black Lives Matter and the MeToo movements have emphasized resilience and healing in the midst of oppression and bigotry. Be it the campaign for equity, promoting social-emotional learning, closing the opportunity gap, or improving school safety, movements in education can reinvigorate people, spawn action, and change lives.

In 2010, entrepreneur and author Derek Sivers gave a TED Talk called "How to Start a Movement." Sivers uses video from a music festival to show how a conversation can be turned into a movement in less than three minutes. If you're not one of the seven million–plus viewers who have watched Derek Sivers's (2010) TED Talk, it's definitely worth a look (see https://bit.ly/1swHBXZ).

As Sivers (2010) dissects lessons learned from the video, he notes that people first need the guts to stand out. Without a fire in our belly, we lose our resolve as soon as things become unpleasant. Second, we need to embrace followers as equals. Sivers (2010) points out that "first followers" encourage their friends to join in. Then, "friend followers" emulate other followers. Third, the movement must be public. As more people participate , it becomes less risky. Barriers like shame, fear, and ridicule melt away. In the fourth element, leadership is deglorified. According to Sivers (2010), it's actually followers who create the "let's do this together" experience, not leaders. Finally, the movement establishes alignment. Although everyone doesn't have to agree on everything, everyone does have to agree on the key areas of unity.

Movements are relational. To start a future-focused movement in your building, rely on face-to-face communication. Create virtual communities to rally people around new ideas. Use social media to show others how to follow. Ask questions of activism rather than questions of practice. As followers spread ideas and propose new possibilities, networks naturally widen and milestones emerge. Before long, a ripple effect is underway. Education movements don't simply facilitate change—they demand it.

Conclusion: A New Hope

Old solutions don't solve new problems. Unless we believe that the impetus to change education falls within our sphere of influence, a new narrative of schooling will remain more of a pipe dream than reality. Doing things a particular way because they're comfortable, popular, or habituated is unlikely to further anyone's cause.

Schools are slow-moving entities, while everything outside moves at hyper-speed. The good news is that opportunities for change exist within every building. In fact, a number of schools are already taking advantage of these opportunities, despite challenges and adverse conditions.

Every school is a living community of people (adults and students) with unique desires, relationships, and circumstances. Teams that invest the time to develop a compelling message and start a movement using the four touchstones in this book will find new sources of hope, energy, and vitality. In essence, they'll be ready for anything!

Appendix

This appendix contains two sample graduate profiles.

1. Carlsbad Unified School District graduate profile (see figure A.1, page 110)
2. Lakeside Union School District graduate profile (see figure A.2, page 111)

Carlsbad Unified School District Graduate Profile

GRADUATE PROFILE

OUR GRADUATES ARE PREPARED FOR SUCCESS

Effective Communicator and Collaborator
Graduates convey their thoughts and responses clearly.
They interact productively to achieve common goals.

Lifelong Learner
Graduates have the passion and vigor for learning that will
fuel them through new opportunities and challenges.

Critical Thinker
Graduates are inquisitive. They notice; they wonder; they
figure things out.

College- and Career-Ready Scholar
Graduates navigate pathways that connect education and
employment to a fulfilling, financially secure life.

Ethical and Responsible Citizen
Graduates display integrity and civic mindedness. They honor
their commitments and aspire to the highest standards.

Self-Directed Individual
Graduates accept responsibility for their learning. They
recognize their strengths and work to their full potential.

Source: Carlsbad Unified School District, n.d. Used with permission.

Figure A.1: Carlsbad Unified School District graduate profile.

OUR VISION OF A
Lakeside Learner

We are preparing our students to be successful with what's next—high school, college, career, and life. Yet the world has changed dramatically over the last hundred years. The Lakeside Student Profile contains the attributes, dispositions, and competencies that will ensure that Lakeside students are prepared for success in their future.

Collaborate Constructively
Students contribute purposefully in teams. They assume various roles and responsibilities with a commitment to shared success.

Think Critically
Students ask questions, use evidence, and reflect on ideas. They seek out complex problems, and are flexible and innovative in designing solutions.

Learn Continuously
Students are passionate to continually learn and grow. They embrace new opportunities that allow them to achieve their goals and dreams.

Communicate Effectively
Students listen and read for meaning. They speak and write with clarity and purpose, adapt to diverse audiences, and when appropriate, incorporate media to enhance ideas.

Care Deeply
Students are kind to others and empowered to make a difference. They listen with empathy and understanding.

Persevere Relentlessly
Students are resilient in the face of obstacles and setbacks. They are determined to achieve success with short-term challenges and long-term goals.

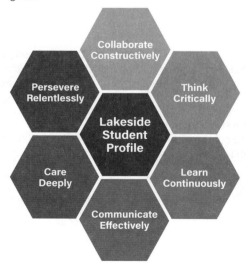

Source: © Lakeside Union School District, 2018. Used with permission.

Figure A.2: Lakeside Union School District graduate profile.

References and Resources

Agarwal, D., Bersin, J., Lahiri, G., Schwartz, J., & Volini, E. (2018). The rise of the social enterprise: 2018 Deloitte global human capital trends. *Deloitte Insights*. Accessed at www2.deloitte.com/content/dam/insights/us/articles/HCTrends2018/2018-HCtrends_Rise -of-the-social-enterprise.pdf on April 10, 2018.

Arruda, W. (2016, September 6). The most dangerous myth about branding. *Forbes*. Accessed at www.forbes.com/sites/williamarruda/2016/09/06/the-most-damaging-myth-about -branding/#705fc625c4fa on May 19, 2019.

Association for Supervision and Curriculum Development. (2011). *Mindset for leading a differentiated classroom*. Alexandria, VA: Author. Accessed at https://pdo.ascd.org/lmscourses /PD11OC137/media/DI-Mgt_M1_Reading_Mindset.pdf on August 25, 2018.

Association for Supervision and Curriculum Development. (2017). Tell me about . . . a personalized-learning challenge. *Educational Leadership*, *74*(6). Accessed at www.ascd.org /publications/educational_leadership/mar17/vol74/num06/A_Personalized-Learning _Challenge.aspx on January 17, 2019.

Bajarin, T. (2012, May 7). 6 reasons Apple is so successful. *Time*. Accessed at http://techland .time.com/2012/05/07/six-reasons-why-apple-is-successful on June 2, 2018.

Billing, K. (2017, March 23). DMUSD dares to think different with District Design. *Del Mar Times*. Accessed at www.delmartimes.net/news/sd-cm-nc-dmusd-design-20170323-story.html on May 18, 2019.

Bock, L. (2015). *Work rules! Insights from inside Google that will transform how you live and lead*. New York: Twelve.

Bowles, N. (2019, April 4). Silicon Valley comes to Kansas. That started a rebellion. *The New York Times*. Accessed at www.nytimes.com/2019/04/21/technology/silicon-valley-kansas -schools.html on May 18, 2019.

Brennan, D. (2018, May 16). Meet the graduating seniors at Sage Creek High School. *The San Diego Union Tribune*. Accessed at www.sandiegouniontribune.com/communities/north -county/sd-no-sage-creek-20180515-story.html on August 3, 2018.

Bryant, A. (2013, June 19). In head hunting, big data may not be such a big deal. *The New York Times*. Accessed at www.nytimes.com/2013/06/20/business/in-head-hunting-big-data-may-not-be-such-a-big-deal.html on May 16, 2019.

Buckingham, M. (2007). *Go put your strengths to work: 6 powerful steps to achieve outstanding performance*. New York: Free Press.

Buckminster Fuller Institute. (n.d.). *Our story*. Accessed at www.bfi.org/about-bfi/our-story on May 15, 2018.

Bunderson, J. S., & Thompson, J. A. (2009). The call of the wild: Zookeepers, callings, and the double-edged sword of deeply meaningful work. *Administrative Science Quarterly*, *54*(1), 32–57.

Carlsbad Unified School District. (n.d.). *Mission, vision, & graduate profile*. Accessed at www.carlsbadusd.k12.ca.us/mvg2 on May 31, 2019.

CBS News. (n.d.). *Celebs who went from failures to success stories*. Accessed at www.cbsnews.com/pictures/celebs-who-went-from-failures-to-success-stories/ on May 15, 2019.

Central Michigan University. (n.d.). *Prepare for success*. Accessed at www.cmich.edu/ess/oss/Documents/Prepare%20for%20Success%20d4.pdf on May 15, 2019.

Chong, A. (2015). Smart power and military force: An introduction. *Journal of Strategic Studies*, *38*(3), 233–244.

Clement, R. (1991). *Counting on Frank*. Milwaukee, WI: Stevens.

Colvin, R. L. (2005). The new philanthropists: Can their millions enhance learning? *EducationNext*, *5*(4). Accessed at www.educationnext.org/thenewphilanthropists on September 9, 2018.

Couros, G. (2015). *The innovator's mindset: Empower learning, unleash talent, and lead a culture of creativity*. San Diego, CA: Burgess Consulting.

Covey, S. R. (1998). *The 7 habits of highly effective families*. New York: Golden Books.

Covey, S. R., Covey, S., Summers, M., & Hatch, D. K. (2014). *The leader in me: How schools around the world are inspiring greatness, one child at a time* (2nd ed.). New York: Simon & Schuster.

David & Lucile Packard Foundation. (n.d.). *Local grantmaking: Children and youth*. Accessed at www.packard.org/what-we-fund/local-grantmaking/children-and-youth/ on June 4, 2019.

d.school. (n.d.). *Shadow a Student Challenge: School leaders take a crash course in empathy*. Accessed at https://dschool.stanford.edu/shadow-a-student-k12 on January 17, 2019.

d.school. (2010). *An introduction to design thinking process guide*. Accessed at https://dschool-old.stanford.edu/sandbox/groups/designresources/wiki/36873/attachments/74b3d/ModeGuideBOOTCAMP2010L.pdf on May 31, 2019.

DuFour, R. (2004). What is a professional learning community? *Educational Leadership*, *61*(8), 6–11.

Dweck, C. S. (2006). *Mindset: The new psychology of success*. New York: Ballantine Books.

Dweck, C. S. (2010). Even geniuses work hard. *Educational Leadership, 68*(1), 16–20.

The Economist. (2016, June 25). *Special report: The return of the machinery question*. Accessed at www.economist.com/sites/default/files/ai_mailout.pdf on March 5, 2018.

Education Elements. (n.d.). *Better schools lead to increases in student enrollment: Racine Unified School District, WI*. Accessed at www.edelements.com/personalized-learning-at-racine-unified -school-district-wi on August 5, 2018.

Education Week Research Center. (2016, September). *Mindset in the classroom: A national study of K–12 teachers*. Bethesda, MD: Author. Accessed at www.edweek.org/media/ewrc_mindset intheclassroom_sept2016.pdf on July 5, 2018.

Eli & Edythe Broad Foundation. (n.d.). *Education*. Accessed at https://broadfoundation.org /education/ on June 4, 2019.

Erdmann, A. (2013, April). *How militaries learn and adapt: An interview with Major General H. R. McMaster*. New York: McKinsey. Accessed at www.mckinsey.com/industries/public-sector /our-insights/how-militaries-learn-and-adapt on April 19, 2018.

Evans, E., & Anderson, R. (2016, July 11). 'Pokemon Go': Craze sweeps the nation and is poised to surpass Twitter. *Los Angeles Times*. Accessed at www.latimes.com/nation/la-na -pokemon-go-20160711-snap-story.html on August 5, 2018.

Every Student Succeeds Act of 2015, Pub. L. No. 114-95, 20 U.S.C. § 1177 (2015).

Fadel, C., Bialik, M., & Trilling, B. (2015). *Four-dimensional education: The competencies learners need to succeed*. Boston: Center for Curriculum Redesign.

Fallbrook Union Elementary School District. (n.d.). *Our superintendent*. Accessed at www.fuesd.org/apps/pages/index.jsp?uREC_ID=779679&type=d&pREC_ID=1175301 on May 14, 2019.

Ferlazzo, L. (2012, October 15). *Response: Classroom strategies to foster a growth mindset* [Blog post]. Accessed at http://blogs.edweek.org/teachers/classroom_qa_with_larry_ferlazzo /2012/10/response_classroom_strategies_to_foster_a_growth_mindset.html on July 5, 2018.

Ferlazzo, L. (2017). Student engagement: Key to personalized learning. *Educational Leadership*, *74*(6), 28–33.

Fleming, K. J. (2016). *(Re)defining the goal: The true path to career readiness in the 21st century*. Los Angeles: CreateSpace.

Friedlaender, D., Burns, D., Lewis-Charp, H., Cook-Harvey, C. M., & Darling-Hammond, L. (2014, June). *Student-centered schools: Closing the opportunity gap* (Research brief). Stanford, CA: Stanford Center for Opportunity Policy in Education. Accessed at https://edpolicy.stanford.edu /sites/default/files/scope-pub-student-centered-research-brief.pdf on August 11, 2018.

Friedman, T. L., & Mandelbaum, M. (2011). *That used to be us: How America fell behind in the world it invented and how we can come back*. New York: Picador.

Gallup. (2017). *CliftonStrengths for students: Your strengths journey begins here*. New York: Gallup Press.

Garcia, E., & Weiss, E. (2017, September). *Education inequalities at the school starting gate: Gaps, trends, and strategies to address them*. Washington, DC: Economic Policy Institute. Accessed at www.epi.org/files/pdf/132500.pdf on August 10, 2018.

Gates, B., & Gates, M. (2018). *Our 2018 annual letter*. Accessed at www.gatesnotes.com/2018 -Annual-Letter on June 4, 2019.

Gino, F. (2016). Let your workers rebel. *Harvard Business Review*. Accessed at https://hbr.org /cover-story/2016/10/let-your-workers-rebel on October 25, 2018.

GivingCompass. (2018, November 14). *Inside a $300 million push to reshape schools.* Accessed at https://givingcompass.org/article/inside-a-300-million-push-to-reshape-schools/ on June 4, 2019.

Gladwell, M. (2002). *The tipping point: How little things can make a big difference.* Boston: Little, Brown.

Gladwell, M. (2008). *Outliers: The story of success.* New York: Little, Brown.

Goldy-Brown, S. (2019). Student loan debt statistics. *Student Debt Relief.* Accessed at www.studentdebtrelief.us/student-loans/student-debt-statistics/ on May 7, 2019.

Gonzalez, J. (2016, September 4). *Using playlists to differentiate instruction* [Blog post]. Accessed at www.cultofpedagogy.com/student-playlists-differentiation on August 12, 2018.

Goodnough, A. (2019, February 19). Kaiser Permanente's new medical school will waive tuition for its first 5 classes. *The New York Times.* Accessed at www.nytimes.com/2019/02/19/health/kaiser-medical-school-free-.html on May 8, 2019.

Goryachev, A. (2018, April 11). *Think like a startup, scale like an enterprise: Balancing the best of both worlds.* Accessed at www.business.com/articles/startup-mindset-enterprise-scaling-business-growth on August 28, 2018.

Grafsgaard, J. F., Wiggins, J. B., Boyer, K. E., Wiebe, E. N., & Lester, J. C. (2013). *Automatically recognizing facial expression: Predicting engagement and frustration.* Accessed at https://people.engr.ncsu.edu/keboyer/papers/grafsgaard-edm-2013.pdf on May 17, 2019.

Great Schools Partnership. (2014). *Stakeholder.* Accessed at www.edglossary.org/stakeholder on May 19, 2019.

Greenthal, S. (2018, November 5). *How Millennial parents are raising their children differently.* Accessed at www.verywellfamily.com/millennial-parents-raising-children-4158549 on October 15, 2018.

Grossman, A. S., Lombard, A., & Fisher, N. (2014). *StriveTogether: Reinventing the local education ecosystem.* Boston: Harvard Business School. Accessed at www.strivetogether.org/wp-content/uploads/2017/03/StriveTogether-Reinventing-the-Local-Education-Ecosystem-314-031.pdf on January 17, 2019.

Hanover Research. (2011, August). *A crosswalk of 21st century skills.* Washington, DC: Author. Accessed at www.montgomeryschoolsmd.org/uploadedFiles/about/strategic plan/21stCenturySkills.pdf on April 30, 2018.

Hardie, E. (2019). Giving teens a place at the table. *Educational Leadership, 76*(8), 18–23.

Healy, M. (2018, August). What should your graduates know? *American School Board Journal.* Accessed at www.nsba.org/newsroom/american-school-board-journal/asbj-august-2018/what-should-your-graduate-know on October 5, 2018.

Heath, C., & Heath, D. (2017). *The power of moments: Why certain experiences have extraordinary impact.* London: Bantam Press.

Heick, T. (2018, August 23). Teaching disruptively. *TeachThought.* Accessed at www.teach thought.com/pedagogy/teaching-disruptively on January 17, 2019.

Hennessey, J. (2018). *Mindsets and the learning environment: Understanding the impact of "psychologically wise" classroom practices on student achievement.* Accessed at http://mindsetscholars network.org/wp-content/uploads/2018/09/Understanding-the-Impact-of-"Psychologically -Wise"-Classroom-Practices-on-Student-Achievement.pdf on July 10, 2019.

IDEO. (2013). *Why design thinking?* [Video file]. Accessed at https://vimeo.com/22570825 on January 17, 2019.

IDEO U. (2015). *Ideation method: Mash-up.* Accessed at www.ideou.com/pages/ideation -method-mash-up on January 17, 2019.

Informing Change. (2017, May). *Expanded learning for California's children: Final evaluation report of the after-school & summer enrichment subprogram's investment strategy.* Accessed at www.packard.org/wp-content/uploads/2017/06/Packard-Expanded-Learning -Evaluation-Report.pdf on June 4, 2019.

Ingersoll, R., Dougherty, P., & Sirinides, P. (2017). *School leadership counts.* Santa Cruz, CA: New Teacher Center. Accessed at https://p.widencdn.net/q1hzuq/Richard-Ingersoll-School -Leadership-Counts on May 14, 2019.

Interactive Schools. (2018, February 8). *50 million users: How long does it take tech to reach this milestone?* [Blog post]. Accessed at http://blog.interactiveschools.com/blog/50-million-users -how-long-does-it-take-tech-to-reach-this-milestone on May 15, 2018.

Irby, M., & Boyle, P. (2014). Aligning collective impact initiatives. In *Collective Insights on Collective Impact* (pp. 15–16). Palo Alto, CA: Collective Impact Forum. Accessed at https://collectiveimpactforum.org/sites/default/files/Collective_Insights_on_Collective _Impact.pdf on September 27, 2018.

Jobs, S. (2005, June 14). *Commencement address: 'You've got to find what you love,' Jobs says* [Speech transcript]. Accessed at https://news.stanford.edu/2005/06/14/jobs-061505 on August 27, 2018.

Jones, L. (2014). *Choosing a college major based on your personality: What does the research say?* Accessed at www.careerkey.org/pdf/choosing-a-major-with-personality-match.pdf on May 16, 2019.

Kania, J., Hanleybrown, F., & Juster, J. S. (2014). Essential mindset shifts for collective impact. In *Collective Insights on Collective Impact* (pp. 2–5). Palo Alto, CA: Collective Impact Forum. Accessed at https://collectiveimpactforum.org/sites/default/files/Collective_Insights_on _Collective_Impact.pdf on September 27, 2018.

Kania, J., & Kramer, M. (2011). Collective impact. *Stanford Social Innovation Review, 9*(1), 36–41. Accessed at https://ssir.org/images/articles/2011_WI_Feature_Kania.pdf on September 25, 2018.

Kelley, T. (2001). *The art of innovation: Lessons in creativity from IDEO, America's leading design firm.* New York: Currency.

Kelly, L., & Medina, C. (2015). *Rebels at work: A handbook for leading change from within.* Sebastopol, CA: O'Reilly Media. Accessed at http://facultylibrary.dmcodyssey.org/wp -content/uploads/2016/04/Rebels-At-Work_sampler.pdf on October 18, 2018.

Lawson, M. A., & Lawson, T. A. (2012). A case study of school-linked, collective parent engagement. *American Educational Resource Journal, 49*(4), 641–684.

Leinwand, P., & Mainardi, C. (2017, September 27). Disruptors and the disrupted: A tale of eight companies—in pictures. *Strategy+Business*. Accessed at www.strategy-business.com /pictures/Disruptors-and-the-Disrupted-A-Tale-of-Eight-Companies-in-Pictures on August 27, 2018.

Levine, D. (2017, January 26). *Building a medical school for team-based care.* Accessed at www.athenahealth.com/insight/building-medical-school-team-based-care on April 19, 2018.

Liesveld, R., & Miller, J. (2005). *Teach with your strengths: How great teachers inspire their students.* New York: Gallup Press.

Lovely, S. (2016, February 23). *Sage Creek High School fosters Genius Project.* Accessed at www.carlsbad.org/124305-2 on January 17, 2019.

Lovely, S. (2017). Build an effective coalition through the 3Es. *Northstar for Principals, 12*(10).

Lovely, S., & Buffum, A. (2007). *Generations at school: Building an age-friendly learning community.* Thousand Oaks, CA: Corwin Press.

Martin, C. (2014, July 5). Shaping a school system, from the ground up. *The New York Times.* Accessed at www.nytimes.com/2014/07/06/business/international/shaping-a-school-system -from-the-ground-up.html on June 14, 2018.

Marx, G. (2014, Fall). Getting students ready for a fast-changing world. *The Source.* Accessed at www.advanc-ed.org/source/getting-students-ready-fast-changing-world on October 30, 2018.

McChesney, C., Covey, S., & Huling, J. (2012). *The 4 disciplines of execution: Achieving your wildly important goals.* New York: Free Press.

Michael & Susan Dell Foundation. (2010, January). *Michael & Susan Dell Foundation funds statewide tools for Teaching Excellence project expansion to five Texas districts.* Accessed at www. msdf.org/press-releases/michael-susan-dell-foundation-funds-statewide-tools-for-teaching -excellence-project-expansion-to-five-texas-districts/ on June 4, 2019.

Miller, R., Latham, B., & Cahill, B. (2017). *Humanizing the education machine: How to create schools that turn disengaged kids into inspired learners.* Hoboken, NJ: Wiley.

National Commission on Excellence in Education. (1983). *A nation at risk: The imperative for educational reform.* Washington, DC: U.S. Department of Education.

NBA Staff. (n.d.). *Legends profile: Michael Jordan.* Accessed at www.nba.com/history/legends /profiles/michael-jordan on May 14, 2019.

Obama, B. (2011). *State of the Union address.* Accessed at www.washingtonpost.com/wp-srv /politics/documents/Obama_SOTU_2011_transcript.html on May 10, 2019.

O'Neill, J, & Conzemius, A. (2006). *The power of SMART goals: Using goals to improve student learning.* Bloomington, IN: Solution Tree Press.

O'Reilly, T. (2005, September 30). *What is Web 2.0?* Accessed at www.oreilly.com/pub/a/web2 /archive/what-is-web-20.html on May 16, 2019.

Pane, J. F., Steiner, E. D., Baird, M. D., & Hamilton, L. S. (2015, November). *Continued progress: Promising evidence on personalized learning.* Santa Monica, CA: RAND. Accessed at www.rand.org/content/dam/rand/pubs/research_reports/RR1300/RR1365/RAND_RR1365 .pdf on August 20, 2018.

Paquette, D. (2017, August 16). Why are factory workers quitting in droves? "Blue-collar jobs are on the way out." *Chicago Tribune.* Accessed at www.chicagotribune.com/business /national/ct-factory-workers-quitting-20170816-story.html on April 19, 2018.

Patrikakou, E. N. (2008). *The power of parent involvement: Evidence, ideas, and tools for student success.* Lincoln, IL: Center on Innovation and Improvement. Accessed at www.centerii.org /techassist/solutionfinding/resources/PowerParInvolve.pdf on October 19, 2018.

Phi Delta Kappan. (2017). *The 49th annual PDK poll of the public's attitudes toward the public schools.* Bloomington, IN: Author

Pink, D. H. (2009). *Drive: The surprising truth about what motivates us.* New York: Riverhead Books.

Pofeldt, E. (2016, October 6). Freelancers now make up 35% of U.S. workforce. *Forbes.* Accessed at www.forbes.com/sites/elainepofeldt/2016/10/06/new-survey-freelance-economy -shows-rapid-growth on March 15, 2018.

Ponzo, S. (2013). *Accelerating skills development: The Dupont approach.* Accessed at www.dupont.com/content/dam/assets/country-config/images_tool_dss_asktheexpert/Sam %20Ponzo%20expert%20article%20accelerating%20skills.pdf on March 5, 2019.

Rath, T. (2007). *StrengthsFinder 2.0.* New York: Gallup Press.

Reeves, D., & DuFour, R. (2018). Next generation accountability. *AASA School Administrator,* 2(75), 34–36.

Reinhart, M. (2003). *Young naturalist's handbook: Insect-lo-pedia.* New York: Hyperion Books for Children.

Richardson, W. (2017). Getting schools ready for the world. *Educational Leadership, 74*(4), 24–29.

Rickabaugh, J. (2016). *Tapping the power of personalized learning: A roadmap for school leaders.* Alexandria, VA: Association for Supervision and Curriculum Development.

Robinson, K. (2015). *Creative schools: The grassroots revolution that's transforming education.* New York: Penguin.

Rubin, C. M. (2016, November 2). *Schools should prepare students for the world of work, not college entrance exams.* Accessed at www.tes.com/news/schools-should-prepare-students-world -work-not-college-entrance-exams on March 15, 2018.

Sage Creek High School. (n.d.). *Genius project.* Accessed at https://sagecreek-cusd-ca.school loop.com/geniusproject on August 3, 2018.

San Diego County Office of Education. (n.d.). *Work-based learning tools and resources.* Accessed at www.sdcoe.net/innovation/cte/Documents/Continuum%20and%20Definitions.pdf on January 17, 2019.

School Leaders Network. (2014). *CHURN: The high cost of principal turnover.* Accessed at http://iowaascd.org/files/7014/5978/0122/principal_turnover_cost.pdf on May 14, 2019.

Schotter, R. (2006). *The boy who loved words.* New York: Schwartz & Wade.

Shadow a Student Challenge. (n.d.). *Shadow a Student workbook.* Accessed at www.shadowa student.org/ on May 12, 2019.

Shorty Awards. (n.d.). *"Be more dog" 6th annual submission entry*. Accessed at https://shorty awards.com/6th/o2-be-more-dog on April 18, 2018.

Simonds, K. (2015, February 9). *I'm 17* [Video file]. Accessed at www.youtube.com/watch?v=0OkOQhXhsIE on January 17, 2019.

Singh, C. (2016, March 9). *Your leadership legacy: How do you want to be remembered?* [Blog post]. Accessed at www.leaderinme.org/blog/your-leadership-legacy-how-do-you-want-to-be-remembered on January 17, 2019.

Sivers, D. (2010, February). *How to start a movement* [Video file]. Accessed at www.ted.com/talks/derek_sivers_how_to_start_a_movement on January 17, 2019.

SkillScan. (2011). *Holland interest themes exercise*. Accessed at www.skillscan.com/sites/default/files/All%20in%20one%20Assessment%20Exercise%20Client%20Forms%20Final.pdf on January 17, 2019.

Skinner, E., & Belmont, M. J. (1993). Motivation in the classroom: Reciprocal effect of teacher behavior and student engagement across the school year. *Journal of Educational Psychology, 85*(4), 571–581.

Steinmetz, K. (2015). Help! My parents are millennials. *Time, 186*(17), 36–43.

Stoops, T. (2018, February). *Do relocating businesses really care about the quality of schools?* (Research brief). Raleigh, NC: John Locke Foundation. Accessed at www.johnlocke.org/update/do-relocating-businesses-really-care-about-the-quality-of-schools on October 30, 2018.

Strauss, K. (2017, October 16). How the giving habits of the super rich are changing. *Forbes*. Accessed at www.forbes.com/sites/karstenstrauss/2017/10/16/how-the-giving-habits-of-the-super-rich-are-changing on October 14, 2018.

Stuart, T. S., Heckmann, S., Mattos, M., & Buffum, A. (2018). *Personalized learning in a PLC at Work: Student agency through the four critical questions*. Bloomington, IN: Solution Tree Press.

Substance Media. (2015, January 28). *Success in the new economy* [Video file]. Accessed at www.youtube.com/watch?v=zs6nQpVI164 on January 17, 2019.

Syed, M. (2010). *Bounce: Mozart, Federer, Picasso, Beckham, and the science of success*. New York: HarperCollins.

Tate, E. (2018, November 15). 'Dear Mr. Zuckerberg': Students take Summit Learning protests directly to Facebook chief. *EdSurge*. Accessed at www.edsurge.com/news/2018-11-15-dear-mr-zuckerberg-students-take-summit-learning-protests-directly-to-facebook-chief on May 17, 2019.

Tomlinson, C. A. (2017). Let's celebrate personalization: But not too fast. *Educational Leadership, 74*(6), 10–15.

Tucker, M. (2017). Globally ready—or not? *Educational Leadership, 74*(4), 30–35.

Wagner, T. (2008). *The global achievement gap: Why even our best schools don't teach the new survival skills our children need—and what we can do about it*. New York: Basic Books.

Walton Family Foundation. (n.d.). *2020 K–12 education strategic plan*. Accessed at https://8ce8 2b94a8c4fdc3ea6d-b1d233e3bc3cb10858bea65ff05e18f2.ssl.cf2.rackcdn.com/04/ab/555b 3ee54d3792eebaf27a803400/k12-strategic-plan-overview-updated.pdf on June 4, 2019.

Whitehurst, G. J. (2016). Grading soft skills: The Brookings soft skills report card. *Evidence Speaks Reports, 2*(4). Accessed at www.brookings.edu/wp-content/uploads/2016/12/es_2016 1215_whitehurst_evidence_speaks.pdf on October 15, 2018.

Whitman, C. (2017, October 6). The art of making your own weather. *Forbes*. Accessed at www.forbes.com/sites/forbescoachescouncil/2017/10/06/the-art-of-making-your-own -weather on August 15, 2018.

Wilke, D. (2019, February 2). The blue collar drought. *Society for Human Resource Management*. Accessed at www.shrm.org/hr-today/news/all-things-work/pages/the-blue-collar-drought.aspx on May 12, 2019.

Winthrop, R. (2018). *Leapfrogging inequality: Remaking education to help young people thrive.* Washington, DC: Brookings Institution Press. Accessed at www.brookings.edu/book/leap frogging-inequality-2 on August 14, 2018.

Wisconsin Department of Public Instruction. (n.d.). *Accountability report cards.* Accessed at https://apps2.dpi.wi.gov/reportcards/home on August 15, 2018.

Wise, S. (2017, February 1). *How might we reinvent professional development for educators?* Accessed at https://dschool.stanford.edu/news-events/how-might-we-reimagine-teacher- professional -development on May 12, 2019.

Wiseman, L., Allen, L., & Foster, E. (2013). *The multiplier effect: Tapping the genius inside our schools.* Thousand Oaks, CA: Corwin Press.

World of Work (n.d.). *RIASEC model.* Accessed at www.worldofwork.net/the-world-of-work/ on May 17, 2019.

YES Prep. (2018, May 23). *Senior spotlight series: Counting down to Senior Signing Day 2018 with North Central* [Blog post]. Accessed at www.theanswerisyes.org/2018/05/23/senior -spotlight-series-counting-down-to-senior-signing-day-2018-with-north-central on January 17, 2019.

YES Prep Public Schools (n.d.). *YES Prep public schools.* Accessed at www.yesprep.org on May 15, 2019.

Young, D. (2017). *See through a student's eyes with a Shadow a Student Challenge.* Accessed at www.gettingsmart.com/2017/02/shadow-a-student-challenge/ on January 17, 2019.

Young, S. D. (2016, August 26). What kind of K–12 education do Millennials want for their kids? *Consumer Affairs*. Accessed at www.consumeraffairs.com/news/what-kind-of-k-12 -education-do-millennials-want-for-their-kids-082616.html on October 15, 2018.

Zhao, Y. (2018). *What works may hurt: Side effects in education.* New York: Teachers College Press.

Zinsmeister, K. (Ed.). (2016). *The almanac of American philanthropy.* Washington, DC: Philanthropy Roundtable.

Index

A

academics, celebrating, 51–53
accelerate, 25
accountability, 13–14
    innovative cultures and, 29
activities, mutually reinforcing, 87
Advanced Placement (AP), 84
affinity maps, 38
affordability, 67
agendas, common, 87
Alberts, S., 54
algebra, 7
alternative work arrangements, 12
any-collar workforce, 6, 10–12
    blue-collar workers, 11
    camouflage-collar workers, 11–12
    empowering students for, 18
    no-collar workers, 12
    white-collar workers, 10–11
AP. *See* Advanced Placement (AP)
Apple, 33–34
Art of Innovation, The (Kelley), 31
assessment
    of engagement, 81, 82
    focus on strong versus wrong in, 40, 41–44
    soft skills, 101–102
    student interests, 60–61
autonomy, 74, 75–76, 79

B

Baby Boomer parents, 95

backbone support, 87
Be More Dog activity, 37
Be More Dog campaign, 35
Bell, Alexander Graham, 9
Berman, M., 85
best practices, 22
Bezos, J., 106
blue-collar workers, 11
Bock, Laszlo, 8
boredom, 48–49
borrowing ideas and practices, 23–24
brainstorming, 32, 36
    reverse, 57
branding, 106
Buffett, W., 84–85

C

Cahill, B., 83
California Department of Education, 94
camouflage-collar workers, 11–12
Center for Curriculum Redesign, 13–14
CESA. *See* Cooperative Education Service
        Agency #1 (CESA)
challenges, grand, 23. *See also* good struggle
champions, 70
Chan Zuckerberg Initiative, 85, 86
change, pace of, 9, 64
character, 13–14
child prodigies, 58
choice, 75–76
civic responsibility, 8

collaboration
building effective coalitions, 97–98
collective impact and, 84, 86–94
as job skill, 8–9
with Millennial parents, 94–99
mobilizing, 25–26
opening the door to, 99–100
with the outside, 2, 3, 83–103
philanthropy and, 84–86
reboots, 80–81
Sandbox Manifesto on, 98–99
takeaways on, 100–103
work-based learning, 92–94
collective impact, 84, 86–94
conditions of, 87
engagement and, 89–92
models of, 103
college
for all, rethinking, 7, 40
challenges facing first-generation attendees of, 52
Columbia University, 84–85
communication
collaboration and, 87
compelling messages in, 106
creating movements through, 107
innovative cultures and, 30
listening in, 45
with parents, 95
skills for jobs, 8, 13, 14
that resonates with a broad audience, 105–106
welcoming outside voices in, 102
communities of practice, 79
compliance, 74
computer science, 21–22
conformity, 14–16
connections, 51
constructive rebellion, 14–16
conversations, 107
Cook, T., 33
Cooperative Education Service Agency #1 (CESA), 67
Cornwall, R., 54
Covey, S., 45–46

creativity
education for, 13, 14
as job skill, 8–9
personalization and, 70
technology and human, 9–10
critical thinking skills, 8, 13, 14
culture
classroom, growth mindset and, 56–58
creating defining moments, 50–54
focus on strong versus wrong, 40, 41–44
innovative, habits of mind for, 29–30
leadership development in, 44–48
strengths-based, 2, 39–61
takeaways on, 59–61
zookeeper effect in, 48–50
curiosity, cultivating, 49
curriculum
innovative practices with, 21–22
job skills related to, 9
personalization and, 65
textbook-driven, 74
customization. *See* personalized experiences
customized learning paths, 68

D

David & Lucile Packard Foundation, 85
defining design challenges, 32
defining moments, 40, 50–54
Del Mar Union School District, 89–90
Deloitte, 92
design thinking framework, 31–33
differentiation, 77
diminishers, 44
discover, 25
disposable diapers, 77, 79
disruptors and disruption, 26, 70
District Design 2022, 89–90
Dodge, G., 84
Donovan, M., 77, 79
DREAMING acronym, 25–26
Drive: The Surprising Truth About What Motivates Us (Pink), 75
DuPont, 11
Dweck, C. S., 45, 55, 56

E

earthly vs. moonshot schools, 71
Edmondson, J., 89
education
  assessing your school's identity and, 105–106
  common narrative about, 5–6
  conformity and, 14–16
  four-dimensional model of, 13–14
  job preparation in, 6–8
  partnerships in, 30
  philanthropy and, 84–86
  reform of, 6
  rethinking, 5–19
  shifting paradigm of, 6–8
  strengths-based, 40
  technology and, 9–10, 13
  U.S. vs. other countries, 83–84
  work-based learning, 92–94
EdWeek, 56
efficacy, 75–76
Einstein, A., 56
elevation, 50
Eli and Edythe Broad Foundation, 85
empathy, 32
empowerment, 46
energy, 29
engagement, 25–26
  2.0, 74–76
  anchoring in collective impact work, 89–92
  autonomy and, 74–76
  in coalition building, 97
  innovative cultures and, 30
  meter of, 81, 82
  sense of purpose and, 48–50
  strengths versus talents and, 42–44
enroll, 97
EPIC encounters, 75–76
equity, 71–72
expectations, 43–44
  of Millennial parents, 96, 97
explore, 25, 97

F

facial expressions, outcome prediction and, 80
failure, 60
personalization and, 71
Failure commercial, 60
Fallbrook Union Elementary School District, 45–48, 70
family structure, 96
fast followers, 26
feedback, 57–58. *See also* praise
Ferlazzo, L., 63
first followers, 107
fixed mindset, 55
Fleming, K., 17, 18
Ford Foundation, 84
Friedman, T., 9–10
friend followers, 107
Fuller, B., 1
fun factor discussions, 81
Future of Jobs and Job Training, The (Pew Research Center), 91–92

G

Gallup Organization, 42
Gates Foundation, 85, 86
gauge, 26
Genius Projects, 53–54
Gino, F., 16
Gladwell, M., 33
Global Human Capital Trends (Deloitte), 92
goals
  helping students set purposeful, 52
  leadership, 60
  moonshot thinking, 71
  SMART, 49
good struggle, 56, 57–58
Google
  Genius Projects, 53
  hiring practices at, 8–9
grades and grading, 54
graduate profiles, 91–92, 101
grand challenges, 23
growth, 42
growth mindset, 2, 45, 55–58
  misconceptions about, 57

H

habits of mind, 29–30
Hardie, E., 49

Heath, C., 50
Heath, D., 50
Heick, T., 23
helicopter parenting, 95
high school, 5
Hoffer, E., 5
Holland, J., 60–61
Horton, K., 67
Hot Teams, 30–33
"How to Start a Movement" (Sivers), 107
Humanizing the Education Machine (Miller, Latham, & Cahill), 83

I

idea grids, 37
ideation, 32
identity, assessing your, 105–106
IDEO, 24–25, 30–33, 36
imagination, bolstering, 50. *See also* creativity
Initiative Inventory, 27–29
innovation
    characteristics of innovative educators, 23–24
    culture of, 29–30
    fear of, 23, 24–25
    letting go of the old and, 27–29
    philanthropy and, 85–86
    stickiness factor and, 33–34
    strategies to increase, 26–34
    in teaching, 22
    what employers want and, 8–9
Innovation Days, 36
innovative practices, implementing, 2, 21–38
    characteristics of educators and, 23–24
    habits of mind for, 29–30
    Hot Teams and design thinking framework, 30–33
    Initiative Inventory for, 27–29
    practical DREAMING and, 24–26
    stickiness factor for, 33–34
    strategies to increase, 26–34
    takeaways on, 35–38
insight, 50
instinct, 42
Institute for Personalized Learning (IPL), 67–68, 79

intensity, relaxed, 49–50
internet, 9–10
interpersonal development, 6, 91–92
intrinsic value, 48–50
inventory, activities and assignments, 26
involvement, 75–76
IPL. *See* Institute for Personalized Learning (IPL)

J

job postings, 102
job skills
    for a changing economy, 8–9
    graduate profiles on, 91–92
    "ordinary," job market for, 10
    soft, 101–102
    technology and, 9–10
Jobs, S., 79
jobs/employment
    any-collar, 6, 10–12
    middle skills, 7
    outlook for, 91–92
    outsourcing, 10
    preparing students for, 16–17
    schooling paradigm and, 6–8
    skills for the changing economy, 8–9
    student interests assessment and, 60–61
    student mindsets about, 39–40
    technology and, 9–10
    work-based learning, 92–94
Jordan, M., 42–43, 60

K

Kaiser, 10–11
Kania, J., 83
Kelley, D., 30–31
Kelley, T., 30–31
knowledge, 13, 14
Kramer, M., 83

L

labeling, 57
labor markets, 7, 10
    alternative work arrangements and, 12
LaCroix, Damian, 13
Latham, B., 83
Leader in Me model, 45–48

leadership
  developing in teachers and students, 40,
    44–48
  as job skill, 8–9
  in movements, 107
  multipliers vs. diminishers, 44
leadership flashlight activity, 60
Learner Profile Template, 68–69
learner profiles, 68–69
learning, future-ready. *See also* personalized
    experiences
  four-dimensional model of, 13–14
  personalized, 63–82
  rethinking education and, 5–19
  touchstones for, 1–2
  work-based, 92–94
listening, 45

M

Mandelbaum, M., 9–10
Marten, C., 86
Mash ups, 36
McClurg, H., 90
measurement, shared, 87
memory, 48
messages, compelling, 106
messiness, embracing, 24
  innovative cultures and, 30
meta-learning, 14
Michael & Susan Dell Foundation, 85
middle school, 5
middle skills jobs, 7
military, the, 11–12
Millennials, collaborating with, 94–99
Miller, R., 83
mindsets
  challenging conventional, 14, 16
  college for all, 40
  fixed, 55
  growth, 2, 45, 55–58
  innovative practices and, 25
  makeover for, 60
  molding, 40, 55–58
mission statements, 89–92
mistakes, being comfortable with, 24
  focus on strong versus wrong, 40, 41–44

mobilize, 25–26
moments
  defining, 50–54
  sparkling, 50
mommy bloggers, 95
moonshot thinking, 71
motivation
  autonomy and, 75–76, 79
  intrinsic, 54
  personalization and, 64, 65
  zookeeping and, 48–50
movements, starting, 107
multipliers, 44

N

Nagelkirk, P., 88
Nation at Risk, A (National Commission on
    Excellence in Education), 83
National Association of Colleges and
    Employers, 91
National Center for Education Statistics
    (NCES), 71
National Commission on Excellence in
    Education, 83
National Merit Scholarships, 84
NCES. *See* National Center for Education
    Statistics (NCES)
need, 42
networks, 26, 88
next practices, 22
niche marketing, 76–77
no-collar workers, 12

O

O2, 35
observation, 31
outcomes
  facial expressions predicting, 80
  outside partners and, 86, 89
  taking responsibility for, 44
  work-based learning, 92–94
outsourcing, 10
ownership, 86

P

parenting styles, 95
parents

collaborating with Millennial, 94–99
personalization and, 66
recognizing contributions of, 96
shopping for education by, 99
training in effective habits, 46
partnerships. *See also* collaboration
for first-generation college students, 52
at Wiseburn–Da Vinci High School, 30
perception, 75–76
performance gaps, 71
persistence, 77, 79
personality types, 60–61
personalized experiences, 2, 3, 63–82
core components of, 66–69
definition of, 63–64
differentiation vs., 77
engagement and, 74–76
equity gaps and, 71–72
niche approach to, 76–77
parents and, 96
persistence and, 77, 79
questions to kickstart, 64–66
strategies for designing, 69–77
for strengths-based education, 40
takeaways on, 79–82
thinking like a startup, 69–72
vision for, 66
Pew Research Center, 91–92
Phi Delta Kappan, 6
philanthropy, 84–86
catalytic, 87–89
Pink, D., 75
PISA, 84
playlists, custom, 77, 78
Pokémon GO, 76
POL (presentations of learning), 30
Power of Moments, The (Heath & Heath), 50
practice, 58
praise, 56, 57–58
presentations of learning (POL), 30
pride, 50–51
principals, personalization and, 65
priorities, 66
problem finding, 23
problem-solving skills, 8, 91–92
proficiency-based progress, 68

progress, proficiency-based, 68
Project Wonder, 60
prototyping, 32
Public's Attitudes Toward the Public
Schools, 6
purpose
personalization and, 77
promoting sense of, 48–50
shared, 29

R
Rapid-Fire Ideas, 17–18
reach, 25
readiness, evaluating your school's, 18–19
Reagan High School, Milwaukee, Wisconsin,
67–68
rebellion, constructive vs. destructive, 15–16
reciprocity, 29
reform, educational, 6, 84
return on investment (ROI), 68
Rewordify, 41
RIASEC assessment, 60–61
Richardson, W., 77
Rickabaugh, J., 63–64
risk taking, 29
responsible, 56
Robinson, K., 6, 16–17
Rockefeller Philanthropy Advisors, 85
Rosenwald Foundation, 84

S
Sage Creek High School, 53–54
San Diego County, 94
Sandbox Manifesto, 98–99
scalability, 67
schooling, changing paradigm of, 6–8
schools, assessing identity of, 105–106
self-talk, 57
Senior Signing Day, 51–53
serendipity, 52
7 Habits of Highly Effective Families, The
(Covey), 46
shadowing students, 72–74, 75, 80
SIGN acronym, 42
silver bullet approaches, 99
Simonds, Kate, 7

Singh, C., 45, 46

Sivers, D., 107

skills, 13, 14. *See also* job skills

SMART goals, 49

social media, 107

socioeconomic status, 71

soft power tasks, 12

soft skills, 101–102

sparkling moments, 50

spontaneity, 29

SSN. *See* Student Success Networks (SSNs)

stakeholders, 97–98. *See also* collaboration

Stanford University, 72, 86

Stanford University Institute of Design, 31–32

startups, thinking like, 69–72

stickiness factor, 33–34

strategic innovation, 26

strategy, structure vs., 99

strengths, talents versus, 42–43. *See also* culture: strengths-based

StriveTogether, 88–89

structure versus strategy, 99

struggle, good, 56, 57–58

student experience, 22

   purpose and, 48–50

   shadowing a student for, 72–74, 75, 80

   strategies to increase innovation and, 26–34

student loan debt, 7

Student Success Networks (SSNs), 87

students

   assumptions about memory in, 48

   "difficult to teach," 57

   empowering, 46

   interest assessment, 60–61

   labeling, 57

   leadership development in, 44–48

   limitations of, accepting, 43–44

   molding mindsets of, 55–58

   problem-solving by, 57–58

   self-directed, independent learners, 64

   what matters to, 38

success, 42

   creating a path for, 67–68

"Success in the New Economy" video, 18

Summit Learning, 86

sustainability, 67

T

talents, strengths versus, 42–43, 58

Tapping the Power of Personalized Learning (Rickabaugh), 63–64

teachers and teaching

   characteristics of innovative, 23–24

   collaborating with parents, 94–99

   conformity vs. rebellion in, 14–16

   focus on strong versus wrong, 40, 41–44

   future-ready, 13–14

   implementing innovative practices in, 21–38

   leadership development for and by, 44–48

   molding mindsets of, 55–58

   niche activities and, 76–77, 78

   personalization and, 65

   promoting sense of purpose with, 48–50

   talents and strengths of, finding, 42

   zookeeping, 48–50

teamwork

   in customization, 70

   Hot Teams, 31–33

   as job skill, 8

   picking teams for, 71

technology

   change driven by, 9–10, 64

   employee partnerships with, 10

   innovative educator's use of, 24

   lag between education and, 13–14

TED Talks, 107

testing, 32, 51. *See also* assessment

That Used to Be Us (Friedman & Mandelbaum), 9–10

Thoreau, H. D., 21

Thrively strengths assessment, 46

Tipping Point, The (Gladwell), 33

Tomlinson, C. A., 64, 65

touchstones, 1–2

   definition of, 1

   takeaways, 17–19, 35–38, 59–61, 79–82, 100–103

trailblazers, 70

Twitter, 9

U

urgency, sense of, 70–71

U.S. armed forces, 11–12

V

venting, 96
vision statements, 89–92
visionaries, 26

W

Walton Family Foundation, 85
white-collar workers, 10–11
Wilkins, K., 42
Wiseburn–DaVinci High School, 29–30
Wonderment, 60
work-based learning, 92–94
Work-Based Learning Continuum, 93, 100

Y

YES Prep, 52, 53
Young, D., 80

Z

Zhao, Y., 84
zookeeper effect, 40, 48–50

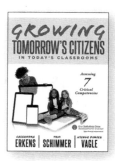

Growing Tomorrow's Citizens in Today's Classrooms
Cassandra Erkens, Tom Schimmer, and
Nicole Dimich Vagle
For students to succeed in today's ever-changing world, they must acquire unique knowledge and skills. Practical and research-based, this resource will help educators design assessment and instruction to ensure students master critical competencies, including collaboration, critical thinking, creative thinking, communication, digital citizenship, and more.
BKF765

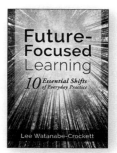

Future-Focused Learning
Lee Watanabe-Crockett
When educators embrace student-centered learning, classrooms transform, learning comes alive, and outcomes improve. With *Future-Focused Learning*, you will discover ten core shifts of practice—along with simple microshifts—that will help take the great work you are already doing and make it exceptional.
BKF807

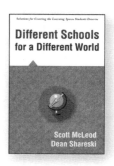

Different Schools for a Different World
Scott McLeod and Dean Shareski
Explore six key arguments for why educators must approach schooling differently: (1) information literacy, (2) the economy, (3) learning, (4) boredom, (5) innovation, and (6) equity. Learn how schools are tackling each argument head-on to prepare students for the demands of the global world.
BKF729

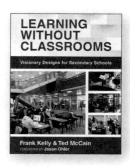

Learning Without Classrooms
Frank Kelly and Ted McCain
Learning Without Classrooms outlines new guidelines for how schools must operate to remain relevant and effective as we move further into the 21st century. The authors detail six crucial elements of schooling and how to address them concurrently to improve secondary schools.
BKF820

Wait! Your professional development journey doesn't have to end with the last pages of this book.

We realize improving student learning doesn't happen overnight. And your school or district shouldn't be left to puzzle out all the details of this process alone.

No matter where you are on the journey, we're committed to helping you get to the next stage.

Take advantage of everything from **custom workshops** to **keynote presentations** and **interactive web and video conferencing**. We can even help you develop an action plan tailored to fit your specific needs.

Let's get the conversation started.

Call 888.763.9045 today.

SolutionTree.com